T0300734

SAVING SAM

SAVING SAM

THE TRUE STORY OF AN AMERICAN'S DISAPPEARANCE IN SYRIA AND HIS FAMILY'S EXTRAORDINARY FIGHT TO BRING HIM HOME

SAM GOODWIN

CENTER
STREET

NEW YORK   NASHVILLE

Center Street
Hachette Book Group
1290 Avenue of the Americas, New York, NY 10104
centerstreet.com
twitter.com/CenterStreet

First Edition: September 2024

Center Street is a division of Hachette Book Group, Inc.

The Center Street name and logo are trademarks of Hachette Book Group, Inc.

The publisher is not responsible for websites (or their content) that are not owned by the publisher.

The Hachette Speakers Bureau provides a wide range of authors for speaking events. To find out more, go to hachettespeakersbureau.com or email HachetteSpeakers@hbgusa.com.

All photos, unless otherwise indicated, are courtesy of the author's personal collection.

Library of Congress Cataloging-in-Publication Data

Names: Goodwin, Sam, 1989- author.
Title: Saving Sam : the true story of an American's disappearance in Syria and his family's extraordinary fight to bring him home / Sam Goodwin.
Description: First edition. | New York : Center Street, 2024.
Identifiers: LCCN 2023055951 | ISBN 9781546007746 (hardcover) | ISBN 9781546007760 (ebook)
Subjects: LCSH: Goodwin, Sam, 1989—Travel. | Goodwin, Sam, 1989—Religion. | Syria—History—Civil War, 2011—Hostages. | Prisoners—Syria—Biography. | Prisoners—United States—Biography. | Travelers—United States—Biography.
Classification: LCC G226.G67 A3 2024 | DDC 956.9104/231 [B]—dc23/eng/20240331
LC record available at https://lccn.loc.gov/2023055951

ISBN: 9781546007746 (hardcover), 9781546007760 (ebook)

Printed in the United States of America

LSC-C

Printing 1, 2024

To my family and lifesaving allies:
Your love and courage made the impossible, possible.

CONTENTS

AUTHOR'S NOTE

On the afternoon of July 26, 2019, within the confines of a government headquarters building in Beirut, I found myself enveloped in the warm embrace of my parents. They had just arrived in Lebanon from St. Louis, marking the end of nine weeks of my complete isolation from both them and the outside world. The watchful presence of dozens of government officials and journalists was gradually beginning to convince me that I had actually survived being held hostage in Syria and was on a path to freedom.

As my parents and I worked to rein in our emotions, I couldn't help but reflect on the tumultuous events I had experienced while inside Syria's gulag archipelago. With a touch of innocence, I remarked to my parents, "I have a story for you." A brief pause followed, during which my mom and dad exchanged a glance before my mom responded, "Well, Sam, we have a story for you too."

When addressing hostage-taking by authoritarian regimes or rogue nonstate actors, my friend and former FBI special agent Ali Soufan often says, "It takes a network to defeat a network." In the case of this book and this story, that couldn't be more accurate. As

I'm sure the CCTV footage inside Lebanon's General Security Directorate headquarters that day would show, the reaction I had to my mom's comment was utter confusion, because, as I would learn, while I was trapped on the *inside*, I had no idea about anything that had happened on the *outside*.

The truth is that only half of this story is mine to tell. The other half is my family's, which is why this book is narrated in first person by multiple characters. In *Apollo 13*–esque fashion, it toggles between me stuck inside a clandestine prison and my family's race-against-the-clock efforts to secure the release of the only American civilian ever freed from Assad regime captivity. You will hear from members of my family, friends, government insiders, and others as we collectively share insight into a saga that includes a journey to every country in the world, celebrities, heads of state, multiple miracles, high-stakes diplomacy, and, most important, what we all learned through this unforgettable experience that we believe can help others today.

This book is more than a record of events. It is a call to empathy, a plea for understanding, and an exploration of the ties that bind us all as fellow human beings. This story is not an isolated incident but a reflection of the broader challenges we face in a world where borders may divide us, but our shared humanity unites us.

—*Sam Goodwin*

NARRATORS

In addition to Sam, below is a list of narrators who share perspectives and stories in first person throughout the book.

TAG Goodwin, Sam's father

Ann Goodwin, Sam's mother

David Goodwin, Sam's youngest brother

Stephanie (Steph) Goodwin, Sam's younger sister

Betty Goodwin, Sam's youngest sister

Stephanie Hajjar, Steph Goodwin's former college roommate

Father Richard Vigoa, pastor at St. Augustine's Parish, Miami

Rob Martini, Sam's close friend

Luke Hartig, former US government official, hostage affairs expert

Joseph Abbas, Lebanese American businessman

SAVING SAM

PROLOGUE

ANN GOODWIN, *Sam's mother*

"**M**om, hurry up!" Sam pleaded as he waved his hockey gear in my face, signaling it was time to leave for practice. "Come on, Mom!"

It was the fall of 1995 in Perrysburg, Ohio. I was struggling to spoon-feed some baby food into the mouth of my youngest daughter, Betty, an infant at the time, before we left, while also trying to move as quickly as possible to please my impatient seven-year-old who wanted to get to the rink. With five kids under the age of eight, getting out the door in these types of situations was often challenging.

As a stalling tactic, I told Sam we weren't going to leave until he taught his other younger sister, Steph, who was three, how to make the sign of the cross. My husband, TAG, and I are devout Catholics and seized every opportunity to infuse religious teachings into the lives of our children.

Sam was annoyed but dutifully started teaching Steph how to make the sign of the cross. "In the name of the Father, the Son, and the Holy Spirit," he repeated to her again and again, touching the tips of her fingers first to her forehead, then to her chest, and then to her left and right shoulders. Steph quickly mastered the hand gestures and the part about the Father and the Son, but she couldn't get her mouth around that last part about the Holy Spirit.

"Mom, she's never going to get it!" Sam cried as I shoveled mush into little Betty's gaping mouth. "I'm going to miss practice!"

"Well, you've got to teach her, Sam, because one day you might need her to pray for you."

PART I

THE ROAD TO DAMASCUS

SAM GOODWIN, *30*

In 1994, a year or so before my attempt to teach Steph the sign of the cross, I made it to the championship round of my third-grade class geography bee. My teacher, Ms. Keller, read the final question: "Name the largest and only Portuguese-speaking country on the continent of South America." For about ten seconds, I visualized the globe next to my bed that my parents had given me, and then I replied, "Brazil." This was the correct answer and earned me a coveted three-night homework pass.

As a kid growing up in northwest Ohio, and later, St. Louis, Missouri, I admittedly wasn't always the best student in school. I cared much more about playing hockey, which is where I put virtually all of my time and effort. But academically, geography was an outlier. An underlying curiosity about the world and its people has existed within me for as long as I can remember. For the majority of my upbringing, though, I suppressed that curiosity, as I didn't really know what to do with it.

Fast-forward nearly two and a half decades to December 31, 2019. I completed a yearslong goal of traveling to every country in the

world. Ironically, my final country was Brazil, which would probably make Ms. Keller proud. I never intended, however, to go to every
country, and now, as years pass and the saga drifts further into the
rearview mirror, the crazier it all seems.

When people hear about my travel journey, and particularly my
experience in Syria, they understandably have a lot of questions.
Why did you want to travel to every country? How the hell did you
fund it all? Did you think going to Syria and other unstable countries would be dangerous? What's your favorite country? Where is
the best food? Furthermore, regarding Syria specifically, there are
plenty of people who consider me to be irresponsible for traveling
there in the first place.

I understand these questions and comments, and I believe the
best way I can respond to them is to share the stories and key events
that shaped my life leading up to the summer of 2019 and to talk
about what travel means to me, how I ended up on a journey around
the world in the first place, and the lessons I've uncovered as a result.

As a teenager in St. Louis in the early 2000s, I continued to have
relative success with hockey and went on to earn a Division I athletic scholarship, a lifelong dream of mine, to Niagara University in
2008. I enjoyed my time in upstate New York and all that being a
student-athlete had to offer. During my senior year, I unfortunately
suffered a serious concussion. I had suffered similar injuries
throughout my playing career, but this one was different. It forced
me to visit neurologists around the United States in search of

answers, but none of them were able to offer much. I was diagnosed with post-concussion syndrome and went on to have a persistent headache every day for eight months. As anyone who's had this type of injury knows, literally and figuratively, it's a dark time.

The headaches didn't subside until after my college graduation in the spring of 2012, when I completed my time at Niagara with dual degrees in communication studies and French, as well as a minor in international business. At the direction of doctors, I decided it wasn't healthy for me to pursue hockey as a career, as another head injury could have led to permanent brain damage. This put me in a tricky spot—I had never considered doing anything else in my life except play hockey and, like many other people in their early twenties, had no idea what I wanted to do.

I began networking, reaching out to my college professors and other contacts in search of my first "big-boy" career move. Among the people I communicated with was a former colleague of my father who was based in Singapore. He responded sympathetically to my concussion debacle and, to my surprise, offered me a marketing internship with his small company in Singapore. When I first received his email, I thought this was silly. "There's no way I would ever actually move to Asia," I thought, but I let that note sit in my inbox for a week or two. As it simmered there, that original underlying curiosity inside me about the world began to rise from its suppressed state.

I talked to my parents about the opportunity, and my father insightfully said to me, "If you go to Singapore and things don't work out, the worst thing that happens is you come home. And you can always do that." In many ways, this safety net and the encouragement from my parents in this situation became the launchpad of my adulthood, and for that I'm thankful.

I moved to Singapore on September 2, 2012. The marketing internship was just okay—it wasn't the best fit for me professionally—but it got me to Asia and opened up an entire new world. Within a week or so of being in Singapore, I learned that there was a hockey league in the tiny city-state, which was an unforeseen discovery given that Singapore is only eighty miles north of the equator, and never in my life had I heard of a hockey player from the country. I gathered some information about the local men's league and learned it was noncontact, meaning there was no body checking. I figured I could play in the league without having to worry about injuring my head. I called my dad and asked him to ship me my gear. He was understandably a bit confused by this request, for the same reasons I was confused that there was any hockey at all. But he boxed everything up, and several days later I was on the ice.

Hockey in Singapore became my primary way of meeting people. The majority of the other players were fellow expats from the United States, Canada, and Europe. A few weeks after I joined the league, one of my teammates, an American man who had been based in Asia for nearly twenty years at that point, told me about a tech start-up company he was launching. We hit it off, and after a few conversations, he offered me a job doing business development and investor relations. I spoke to my internship boss about this opportunity, and he was happy for me and suggested I pursue it. After all, the whole point of the internship in the first place was to obtain some initial experience and get the chance to network. I accepted the new position and went on to work for this start-up for the next six years. Our business developed an online game for young teens, similar to *Minecraft* and *Club Penguin*. It also had a charitable arm, and I helped cofound an NGO that administered humanitarian assistance to impoverished families in the Philippines and Cambodia. The icing on the cake was when my former college roommate, teammate, and friend, Rob Martini, came to Singapore and joined the company too. I loved my job, my colleagues, and the mission of the business.

When I moved to Asia, my original plan was to stay for only about three months, but I ended up living and working there for more than half a decade, from 2012 to 2018. It was a fantastic way to begin my professional career. During those six years, every work meeting I attended, I was the dumbest person in the room. This was uncomfortable but simultaneously a time of huge personal and professional growth. I learned more about business, people, and the real world than I ever could have asked for in an early-career job.

In my free time while living in Singapore, I traveled as much as I could. I was in my midtwenties, had the world's best airport in my backyard, and had occasional flexibility in my work schedule. A personal preference when I traveled was to avoid repeating destinations. Even if I traveled somewhere and had a wonderful experience, on the next weekend or holiday I would try to go somewhere different. In addition, I would also usually travel back to St. Louis for Christmas and in the summer to see my parents and siblings. Given that Singapore is on the other side of the world, I could often choose which direction I wanted to travel around the globe and try to stop in different places for a day or two en route.

After putting this formula into play for six years, I realized in early 2018 that I had visited 120 countries on all six inhabited continents. At this point, I asked myself, "Well, how many countries are there?" For me, travel was always about experiences and connecting with people and never about ticking boxes or checking places off a list. I did some research and learned that there are 193 fully recognized UN sovereign states. I then thought to myself, "Wow, maybe I could go to all of them." The competitive athlete in me likes setting goals and working toward achieving them.

This kicked off months of research. I learned that, at the time, there were only about a hundred people who had been to every country and became fueled by the idea of joining this exclusive group. For reference, roughly 600 people have been to outer space. Money was a huge consideration. I had spent the past six years working and had no kids or spouse. I calculated that I had just enough money saved to allow me to travel to the remaining seventy-ish countries, if I traveled wisely and on a budget.

Simultaneously, as I was doing all of this research in my spare time, the start-up company, which I had helped grow to thirty-plus staff across four countries, was seemingly facing some uncertainty, as so many start-ups do. I had also now been in Singapore for quite some time, and although I loved it and to this day consider it a second home, I was getting a bit antsy and ready for something new.

I ran the calculations countless times in my head, and it always led back to this burning desire to try to visit the rest of the countries in the world. I wanted to continue learning through travel, but I also wanted to work toward achieving something I thought was extraordinary. Some people, even members of my immediate family, thought I was being unrealistic for considering this quest. I knew it was possible I could fail. I might run out of money. I might not be able to get certain visas. I had internal questions about the security situation in some areas of the world and knew I would need to be extra diligent. But I feared regret more than I feared failure, and in the summer of 2018, I decided I was going to give it a shot.

I determined that I could probably travel to the rest of the countries in approximately one year. Once I finished, I was going to go straight back to my career. This was the deal I made with myself, and it was also what I truly wanted. I didn't want to be a nomad forever and wander aimlessly—there's nothing wrong with that, it just wasn't for me. I had a set goal, and I had a plan. I figured that if I didn't try now, I might never get another chance. So I went for it. I left Singapore. I left my job. The underlying curiosity that had lived within me since I was a kid at that geography bee had gotten the best of me, and I was off.

For the next nine months or so, I based myself in Dubai, staying with a friend there since it was geographically closer to many of the places I hadn't visited yet—primarily in Africa. While in Dubai, I set up a small business giving ice skating lessons to kids of expats based in the United Arab Emirates. It wasn't sustainable, but it did give me some extra money and allowed me to meet new people. The majority of these months, however, I was not physically in Dubai. I was on the road.

During this time, my style of travel shifted. This was because my overall goal with travel had temporarily changed too. I didn't always spend as much time in each country as I potentially would have preferred had I not been on a quest to visit all of them. There were also some places, like Chad, for example, where I only spent a couple days and when I departed, I didn't feel like I needed any more time. I measured what counted as a visit not with a clock but with experiences. For the record, I did not count airport visits and also did not count just stepping over a border and stepping back. All of this can get very arbitrary and people in the "extreme travel" community often fiercely debate it.

In summary, I did the best I could. I didn't have unlimited time or money and was trying to complete this goal and get back to my "real life." It was a constant balance and, like any worthwhile venture or endeavor in life, required many compromises, detours, and trade-offs. Despite these challenges, I loved my quest and was determined to complete it.

By the late spring of 2019, I was closing in on my goal, having traveled to approximately 170 of 193 countries, blogging about each of them along the way. I was in the South Pacific island nation of Tuvalu when the trajectory of my travel journey veered in an unexpected direction.

ANN GOODWIN, *Sam's mother*

"I'm talking to my mom."

Those were the last words I heard Sam say before he vanished into thin air.

It was nine in the morning on May 25, 2019. I was in a car with my two daughters and Bridgid, my future daughter-in-law, heading to a lifelong friend's house for a wedding celebration in Michigan, about an hour west of Detroit. It was beautiful weather that Memorial Day weekend. My husband—Thomas Aquinas Goodwin, known to the world simply as TAG—and my other sons, Paul and David, had gone off for a round of golf with the other men in the wedding party. We're a family of seven, three boys and two girls, and everyone was there except for Sam.

Sam had gone to Syria.

Not Syria, Indiana, or Syria, Virginia. Syria, the country in the Middle East. Although this was the nation that had endured a civil war for seven years by the time Sam went there, I found comfort when he explained to me that he was traveling with a guide to the safest area of the country, an area controlled by US-backed Kurds and three hundred miles from any ongoing conflict.

Traveling the world had become a means for Sam to satisfy his curiosity about people. Even as a young boy, Sam was inquisitive about how people lived in other parts of the world. We traveled quite a bit as a family. We'd been to Europe a couple of times when the kids were teenagers, and TAG and I had traveled to a number of other destinations with one or more of them in recent years, including South Africa, Istanbul, and the Galápagos Islands. We'd even been to the Winter Olympics in Sochi, in Russia, since we are a family that enjoys ice hockey.

But Sam had really taken to it since he'd moved to the Far East. Singapore is an international travel hub, so he'd started touring the region—Thailand, Vietnam, Malaysia, Japan, China. He would also come back home every summer to visit us and would stop off along the way to explore new places. Since Singapore is pretty much on the opposite side of the globe from St. Louis, he had lots of long-layover options. After several years, he realized he'd been to over a hundred countries. And that was when he began wondering—how many countries *are* there in the world? And was it possible to visit them all?

TAG and I knew that Sam was a responsible and smart young man, not to mention a very determined one. He had now taken all the goal-oriented drive of a competitive athlete and applied it to this new journey. I guess that's what makes Sammy run.

The experience of travel had proven over the years to be very meaningful for Sam but also fascinating for us too. As a family, we've always been extremely close, so Sam would go out of his way to include us in his adventures. He made sure to call from wherever he went. Often he would hold up his phone on FaceTime so we could see the place he was visiting. Over the years, we'd gotten used to calls from strange and exotic places, and Sam's reports were usually extremely encouraging. No matter where he was—be it Germany, Pakistan, Chile, or Azerbaijan—people were notably friendly and welcoming. It was heartwarming to hear this, especially because so much of the mainstream news from these places can be negative.

"There are just great people all around the world," Sam would tell me. "Some places, one percent of the people are ill-intentioned, and they sometimes happen to be in control. But most of the people in the world are wonderful and kind." As parents, we were somewhat uneasy about Sam going to Iran, but he met a lovely young couple with a baby on Kish Island who took him home for dinner and made him feel very welcome. Sam also didn't just travel as a tourist. Whenever possible, he made an effort to give back to the local communities he visited, like digging wells in northern Nicaragua, supporting rice farmers in rural Cambodia, or simply playing with village kids in the hills of Rwanda. He always tried to leave places better than he found them.

Although he'd been denied a career in hockey, Sam often used those skills as a bridge to reach other cultures. He coached the Singapore national hockey team for five years, taking them to international tournaments around Asia, and later gave skating lessons to kids in Dubai. Sam was a connector. Without people like him, the world would be a poorer, less understanding place.

For sure, he'd had some close calls on his travels, not because of negligence on his end but because these types of things are inevitable when traveling to every country in the world. The day after he flew out of Libya, rebel planes bombed the airport. He'd also encountered gang riots in Haiti and militiamen riding on gun trucks in the streets of Mogadishu. By that Memorial Day weekend in 2019, though, he had traveled to 180 countries. Sam was a resourceful and seasoned traveler who took every precaution he could, and he was nearing the end of his journey.

Still, this was Syria. I didn't know much about the Middle East, but I knew there was generally some level of civil unrest in the country. So I'd been very relieved earlier that morning when Sam had sent me a brief video clip of him at a shawarma stand—one of his favorite foods—on a very quiet-looking street in Syria. "Kebabs are 75 cents in Iraq but only 50 cents in Syria," he wrote next to footage of a man slicing lamb off a rotating grill.

Later, when my phone buzzed again and Sam's name flashed up on the screen, all seemed to be well.

I was sitting in the passenger seat of the car. As my son's face appeared on the screen, I held up the phone so that the girls in the back could see and talk to him too. Sam was in a small town called Qamishli, which was very close to the Turkish and Iraqi borders, and which was under Kurdish control. He was on his way, he said, to meet a local guide who would show him safely around the town and surrounding area.

We chatted for a few minutes, and Sam told us how happy he was to finally be there. He said he was sorry to be missing out on the wedding, which for the Goodwins was also a chance for a big family get-together.

"Hey, pan over the landscape for me," I said, as I always did when Sam was in a new place, so that we could see what he was seeing. He moved the screen slowly across a street of low-rise buildings and Middle East–style apartment houses. In addition, there were locals drinking tea at sidewalk cafés and shopping at outdoor markets. We looked at the scene, saying that it appeared to be quite a nice place. Then we heard a muffled shout from somewhere off camera.

"I'm talking to my mom," Sam told someone we couldn't see.

The image spun and blurred, and the line went dead.

That moment still haunts me, even all these years later.

It wasn't unusual for the line to go dead when Sam called from a remote location where the internet was unreliable or the telephone network might just randomly cut out. I tried to shrug off the unexpected interruption as we drove to the wedding, so as not to spoil the mood for the happy couple and their guests. But it was always there, gnawing at me, no matter how much I tried to suppress it. In any case, there seemed to be nothing to do but wait for Sam to call back, which I tried to convince myself he would do as soon as he found a better connection.

SAM GOODWIN

By the spring of 2019, the conflict in Syria seemed to be in a period of remission. The regime of President Bashar al-Assad was grinding down the opposition with the aid of Russian airstrikes, Iranian gold, and Hezbollah guerrillas from neighboring Lebanon.

I won't say that going to Syria was necessarily comfortable, because after all, it was still Syria. But the entry process was formal and well organized compared with some other places I had visited. In December 2018, for example, I walked into Sierra Leone. I was surprised when a shirtless man sitting in a lawn chair by the road suddenly asked me for my passport. It turned out *he* was the border guard.

The Kurds, by contrast, had a series of well-run checkpoints across the border region with Iraq, where I had spent the previous week, securing the documentation needed to pass through Kurdish-controlled territory. As I went through each checkpoint, an immigration official checked my passport and then waved the taxi through.

A strange twist of fate had brought me to the small, dusty town of Qamishli, a place that few people outside of Syria have probably ever heard of. Several weeks earlier, on May 2, I was in the midst of a trip across the Polynesian micronations of the South Pacific and spending the night in Tuvalu, a collection of tiny islands located midway between Hawaii and Australia. That evening, I walked past a live music performance in a park and noticed a young blond woman playing on the covered stage. It was a small affair, but the woman was great, so I listened for a while, reflecting on how cool it was that I could bump into a live music gig on an island in the middle of the Pacific Ocean. Eventually, I went back to my backpacker hostel. The following morning, I was on a flight to the next stop, which happened to be Fiji, another 750 miles to the south. There, on the plane, was the blond woman who'd been playing in the park the night before. As she was boarding, I heard one of her traveling companions call her by her name—Joss. That was when it clicked. This was Joss Stone, the Grammy Award–winning British singer. I was only modestly familiar with her music; I knew her more because of the traveler grapevine. She was also on a mission, not just to visit every country in the world but to play a gig in every one of them too. She called it her Total World Tour. That was what had brought her to these remote islands—the same restless ambition I had, combined with a lot more musical talent.

When we got to Nausori Airport in Suva, Fiji, I was ahead of her in the immigration line, which snaked back and forth on itself. As we passed each other, I nodded hello and asked, "How many countries have you visited?" She looked pleasantly surprised and said she was at 170 or something like that. I replied, "Oh yeah, me too, I'm doing the same thing." As the line weaved forward, we kept passing each other and chatting, until I went through passport control, grabbed my bag, and went to the lobby to wait for my connecting flight to Nadi, a town on the other side of Fiji. A few minutes later, Joss and a couple members of her team came out of immigration. She walked straight over to me, sat down at my table, and said, "I want to interview you!"

Her enthusiasm for travel was boundless and we instantly hit it off. She whipped out her cell phone and started recording some of our conversation about the places we'd been and the things we'd seen and done. The video interview went on for about seven minutes. Joss is a warm and positive person—it's part of her presence, both on and off the stage—and she seemed genuinely interested in what motivated me to travel and what takeaways I had from my years on the road. It was all very chill, just two travelers sharing their experiences. It was easy to overlook the fact that she was a global superstar.

Inevitably, we swapped tips and contacts for places we were still trying to visit. For Iran, I suggested she go to Kish Island, a place I had been to three years earlier, instead of the mainland, as it's logistically simpler for Westerners. I also gave her contacts for my fixers in Yemen and Libya, both of which I had already visited and where I had wonderful experiences despite each of the nations experiencing their own breeds of instability.

Joss was very pleased and in return asked if I had any "challenging" countries remaining on my journey. I told her Syria was probably the toughest one I had left and that I was still in the process of my usual research and due diligence to determine the best way to travel there.

"I was just in Syria two months ago!" she said. "I went in through Kurdistan! I can connect you with my fixer."

At that point, I hadn't really considered going to Syria through Kurdistan. In fact, if anyone had mentioned Kurdistan, I would have probably assumed they were talking about the northern region of Iraq, an area I had visited about six months earlier, which borders Syria and has its own government. But the Kurds are spread out across northern Iraq, Iran, Syria, and up into southeastern Turkey. In fact, it is the largest ethnic group in the world that does not have its own country, and Kurds frequently complain about how often they have been betrayed, ignored, or attacked by regional and global powers. "The only friends the Kurds have are the hills," is an old saying in the region, where fighters often have been forced to take to the Zagros Mountains to wage guerrilla warfare against foreign occupiers. Saddam Hussein used chemical weapons against them in the 1980s, wiping out whole villages. In Iraq, they have their own armed forces, and in Syria, Kurdish militias have carved out a few safe havens, keeping the Assad regime and the Islamic State fanatics at bay.

Back in February, Joss told me, she had played a small concert in a Kurdish-controlled corner of northeastern Syria. It had been in a tiny town called Derik, very close to the Iraqi border. Her audience in the cold and damp hall had only been around seventy people, mostly women and kids, in addition to some two dozen members of the Kurdish military. There was also a former British soldier who was happy to hear a familiar voice out there in the desert.

For Joss, who got her first break as a thirteen-year-old singing on a BBC talent show, it was an incredibly moving experience, and it resonated closely with my own. She had gone to a distant corner of the planet and had found a close-knit community that welcomed her with open arms. Crucially for me, she also had the name of a reputable local fixer, an Erbil-based Kurdish man named Simon Khayat, who was well known for guiding foreign journalists and travelers in unfamiliar environments. Joss had met Simon through the British photographer and journalist Paul Conroy. Paul, a close friend of Joss, had accompanied her on her trip to Syria, making his first return to the country since 2012.

As it turned out, Joss and I were both waiting in Suva for the same connecting flight, so we sat in the airport for a couple of hours, chatting as easily as old friends about our shared passion. I don't think we even mentioned her music once, except in the context of the strange places she had played gigs on her world tour. She was financing it herself, often performing with local musicians in a garden, a forest, or sometimes as part of an organized music festival, but also highlighting local charity work and generally trying to "meet good people and do good things," as she said.

As we took our seats on the flight to Nadi, we promised to keep in touch. When I got to my hostel that evening, I immediately sent a WhatsApp message to Simon. In my experience, following the path of other travelers ahead of me had always been among the best ways to ensure a positive experience. I sent Simon a selfie of Joss and me smiling together at the Suva airport—her looking like a million bucks despite the fact that she'd been in transit for hours, and me just looking like a disheveled traveler. "I am on a quest to travel to every country in the world and have yet to travel to Syria. I have only a few countries remaining and am wondering if you might be able to help me visit Syria?"

If he hadn't worked so recently with Joss on her gig in Derik, Simon would probably have thought I was a madman. Most of the foreigners he dealt with were reporters, so I also sent him a link to my travel blog on Instagram. Five minutes later, he wrote back. He was ready to help me at any time. A thrill of excitement shot through me in that little hostel room in Nadi. This is what it was all about—new places, unexpected connections, and a deeper understanding of the world.

I spent the next few weeks doing due diligence and working with Simon on the details of the trip. Throughout my travels, safety was always the top priority, as much as it can be on a quest like this. I don't think it's cool to be in unsafe situations and I don't go looking for trouble. I was, however, committed to completing my travel journey, one that often required a great deal of creativity and resourcefulness.

On May 25, 2019, with the help of Simon and continued logistical support from Joss, both of whom had been incredibly helpful, I crossed into Syria by land from Iraq, caught a taxi, and headed into the country.

⌒

The town of Qamishli lies right on Turkey's southern border, but I couldn't enter from Turkey. Instead, I had to go in from the Iraqi side, a drive of about fifty miles. I had spent the previous five days in Erbil obtaining all the necessary papers and documentation. I met with several of Simon's friends who helped me with these documents, as they knew the ins and outs of the regional landscape. In my downtime, as I waited for various permissions and approvals, I either explored the city or relaxed in my hotel room, usually watching the St. Louis Blues on TV, my hometown NHL team, who were on the verge of beating the San Jose Sharks and advancing to the Stanley Cup Final for the first time in nearly fifty years. Despite being on the road, I tried to watch these games when I could.

The Kurds I'd met had all been very welcoming. I enjoyed hanging out in the markets of the five-thousand-year-old city, its center built on a vast earthen mound formed from its ruined predecessors, piled up by generations of conflicts dating back to Mesopotamia and the Assyrian Empire.

Kurdistan is a dry, dusty place, hemmed in by Turkey, Iran, and Iraq. But in spring, the grass and flowers briefly flourish, giving it an almost alpine feel. Then the summer heat dries out the rocky valleys and hills and it feels like the Middle East again. It was already getting hot in May, but the hills were still pretty. My taxi driver, arranged by Simon, drove me across the country, a peaceful and relaxing ride. We soon arrived at the Syrian border, a place known as Faysh Khabur, marked by the Tigris River with the Kurds controlling both sides. As we stopped at the first of several checkpoints, a Kurdish soldier came out of an office and inspected my passport and travel permit and logged the details in his computer. He then waved me on, an uneventful way to enter a new country. I crossed to the Syrian side of the river and went inside another office. I gave the immigration officer my passport. He inputted my information into his computer and then stamped a white piece of paper authorizing my entry.

I was excited to be in Syria, a place I had been wanting to visit for years. I jumped in a taxi and within a few minutes flashed past Derik, the small town where Joss had played her Syrian concert a couple of months before. From there, it took roughly two hours to get to Qamishli, where Simon had recommended I visit.

Qamishli is an unremarkable desert town. Low-rise, tawny apartment blocks line neatly laid-out streets, some of them lined with pines for shade. The town was founded in the 1920s, both as a railway depot and as a refuge for Assyrian Christians who had fled the Ottoman genocide. Now it is an Assyrian and Kurdish city that has both a large Christmas celebration every year and a Kurdish Muslim new year festival of Nowruz. May 25 was a Saturday, and I had done my research and was planning to attend Mass the following morning at the Armenian Catholic church near my hotel. Qamishli had been largely spared from the conflict in Syria, and by the time I arrived, it was peaceful, a relative safe haven for the administration of the self-ruling northeastern enclave.

I had a reservation at the Asia Hotel, a spare but clean establishment. It was often used by Western journalists. The plan was that I would meet a friend of Simon's at a restaurant a short walk from the hotel. By the time I checked in, I was hungry, so I stepped out onto the street to grab a shawarma from a grill next door. Eating shawarma, which I often characterize to friends in the United States as Middle Eastern Chipotle, was the first thing I did in every Middle Eastern country I visited. No one I encountered, including the hotel receptionist, spoke any English, and nobody reacted strangely to a new foreign traveler in their presence. After having been to so many unfamiliar places, I had developed a sense as to when I stood out uncomfortably, and my radar was not sounding any sort of alarm here.

Back in my room, I called my close friend Rob Martini. Rob and I had been roommates at Niagara University and had played hockey together. He had even moved to Singapore for a few years, where we had done a lot of traveling throughout Southeast Asia and beyond. Since then, our lives had gone in different directions. Rob had moved back to his hometown of Toronto to work for a private investment firm, and he and his wife were in the process of buying a house, while I was in a cheap hotel room in Syria. Nevertheless, we talked for almost an hour on the phone about my trip, his impending purchase, and some details of my plans for the next few days. I gave him the phone number of my fixer, Simon, and a copy of my travel permits, just in case I happened to have any issues.

Before I left Erbil, Simon had given me his local Syrian SIM card with unlimited data for my trip, so I took out my cell and recorded a brief video for my family of me eating the delicious meat sandwich. Then I went back to the hotel and waited until it was time for my meeting with Simon's friend.

He'd told me to meet him in a restaurant about three hundred meters down the road. The plan was that we'd have a meal and then he would show me some of the sites around the town, including some of the churches. As a Catholic, I was looking forward to that and hoped to show it to my mom, who is a very spiritual person. I was planning to spend two nights in Qamishli and head back to Iraq on Monday morning. From there, I had a flight booked from Erbil back to the United States, as the remaining twelve countries of my quest were all in the Americas.

As I walked down the street to meet my guide, I passed a roundabout with a white stone statue of Hafez al-Assad, a man who looked more like a 1950s provincial bank manager than the former bloody dictator of Syria who had killed tens of thousands of his own people, just like his son who's now ruling the country. It was at that point that I decided to call my mom, who I knew would be driving to the wedding right at that moment and would be reassured to hear from me. She picked up almost immediately. I told her I was in Syria and that all was well.

Since I had a local SIM card from Simon with unlimited data, I decided to FaceTime my mom instead of a normal phone call to make her even more comfortable. "Hey Sam, pan over the landscape for me," she said, curious as ever to know what the place looked like. I held up my phone and started showing her the statue and the roundabout.

As we were talking, a man's voice called out in my direction in a foreign language. I looked to my right, and there was a soldier coming toward me from the other side of the street. A handful of other men in uniform emerged behind him from the other side of the roundabout. I had not seen them before and didn't know who they were.

I had traveled to various places in the world where photography was not allowed, sometimes for military reasons, like in certain areas of North Korea, but also for more traditional reasons like at the Sistine Chapel in Rome or in many Japanese temples. In order to assure these men that I was not trying to take photos of anything I wasn't supposed to, I shouted to them, "I'm talking to my mom," clearly, assuming their mastery of English would be limited at best. I was respectful, as I always am in such situations. I'm not doing anything wrong here, I told myself, so just be patient, smile, relax, and take a deep breath. I'm not a rule-breaker by nature, and in any case, I knew that playing the angry American tourist in a place like this certainly wouldn't serve me well. The first soldier grabbed the phone out of my hand. Another demanded my passport and then they hustled me across the road in the direction from which they had just come. Within thirty seconds, a black pickup pulled up next to us and two more armed men in uniform jumped out. I was pushed into the back seat, and we sped off. I was scared, confused, and had no information or anyone to help. I was desperately trying to understand what was happening. Less than a minute later, we stopped at what appeared to be some sort of military compound. I was hustled out of the vehicle and taken into an office where a guy in a white soccer jersey started questioning me in not-very-good English.

It may sound strange, but at that point I wasn't overly worried. The guy who was questioning me wasn't particularly aggressive, though with his basic English, he had trouble understanding my responses to his questions and why I was in Syria. I told him I was writing an online blog about my travels, which might have been hard enough to explain even to someone with more advanced English. I saw that one of the soldiers standing by the wall had my phone and was scrolling through it. I told them to look at my blog site, but the soccer jersey man was clearly not interested. I said I'd been on my way to meet my guide at a restaurant that was only a five-minute walk from where we were sitting, but this, again, all seemed to fall on deaf ears.

This frustrating back-and-forth discussion went on for nearly three hours and became progressively more uncomfortable. Then, the soccer jersey man pulled out a digital camera and a small whiteboard. He wrote something in Arabic and handed it to me. I asked him what it said. He replied, "Samuel Robert Goodwin," the full name on my passport. He told me to stand against the wall and hold it in front of me while he took a picture.

With a sinking feeling, I realized this was a mug shot.

With the picture taken, I was led out into the hall and past a line of soldiers on either side of the corridor. Then I was taken outside to a waiting van. Some of the soldiers got in with me and others followed in a car as the vehicle drove out of town and into the desert.

By this point, I was starting to feel very uncomfortable. Something was going seriously wrong and I had no way of understanding what it was. After a twenty-minute ride, a Syrian military compound lined with barbed wire and concrete fences appeared out of nowhere in a field. We pulled in. Another, larger detachment of armed soldiers was waiting in the courtyard. As I got out, it dawned on me that they had all been waiting just for me.

For the first time, with a sense more of fatality than fear, I thought to myself, "Is this where my story ends?"

ANN GOODWIN

We drove back from the wedding on Sunday, just TAG and me. The kids had headed off to a nearby lake house to spend the rest of the Memorial Day weekend with friends by the water. It was a relief to now be in the car with just TAG because I didn't have to cover up my growing concern. I'd texted Sam before I went to bed the night before, telling him I was getting worried and that he should call, text, or email me no matter what time it was. Given the time differences, he was always very respectful not to wake me up with a phone call or a pinging text message in the middle of the night.

We have a family text message group, called FAMJAM, so I asked the kids if anyone had heard from Sam on Instagram or Facebook or any of the other social media platforms with which I'm not really familiar. No one had, which further fueled my increasing concern. Since the inception of the FAMJAM group chat roughly a decade earlier, its title has also included an emoji of a frog, which is an acronym for "fully rely on God" and serves as an important daily reminder to our family. As Sam's silence persisted, I was beginning to sense a forthcoming surge of this subtle emoji's significance. TAG was still insisting everything was going to be fine, that there was some harmless explanation for Sam's blackout. I wasn't convinced, but for now I had to bite my tongue. The drive back to St. Louis was a long and uncomfortable ordeal for me.

I woke up very early on Memorial Day and was not in a good place.

When TAG got up, he suggested we go for a long hike to enjoy the spring weather and take my mind off Sam. During our thirty-five years of marriage, my husband and I have developed certain behavioral patterns, one of which is that I am usually the first to start worrying about something. TAG typically tries to reassure me that everything will work out fine, which, frankly, it usually has. But this time, as we walked through the woods and he told me not to worry, it just wouldn't wash.

"You say it's too soon to start worrying," I said, probably rather too brusquely. "So, tell me, when exactly will you be worried? Because I'm worried about Sam now."

TAG thought about it for a moment. "Let's give it twenty-four hours," he said. "If we don't hear from Sam for the rest of the day, then by noon tomorrow we'll do something about it."

We carried on walking, and maybe it was the fresh air and the exercise and the promise that we now had a deadline, but that calmed me down a bit. Somehow I managed to get through the rest of the day and went to bed as usual around nine thirty or so. But I couldn't rest. I lay awake for hours, with TAG gently sleeping beside me. I couldn't stop thinking about Sam and where he might be right at that moment and what might have happened to him. By midnight, I couldn't stand it anymore and definitely knew I wasn't going to make it to TAG's deadline of noon the next day.

I got up and went to my laptop. We have become so reliant on Google searches these days for all our quick answers that my first impulse was to sit down and type in, "My son is missing in Syria, what do I do?" I thought every Google search comes up with some sort of an answer, but perhaps not surprisingly, there was none for that one. I was in totally new territory.

I remembered when TAG and I had been hiking earlier that day, I'd asked him what he planned to do when his self-imposed deadline ran out. He said he guessed he would start by reaching out to the State Department. Now, I consider myself to be an educated person, and do in fact serve as the president of a Catholic high school in St. Louis, but my understanding of how the government works is pretty minimal. At that time, I could have named only one of my state's senators, would have been hard-pressed to tell you the difference between an embassy and a consulate, and probably knew less about the workings of our federal government than a ninth grader in my own school. Nevertheless, it was obvious that no government agency in DC would be open in the middle of the night, so I got back on the computer and started searching online for the US embassy in Syria.

There was a website for the embassy, but it told me that the actual embassy had closed in 2012, when the US government broke off all diplomatic ties with the Assad government. There was also a message from the State Department, which runs the US overseas missions, saying that any inquiries about US citizens inside Syria should be addressed to the US embassy in neighboring Iraq or the US consulate in Erbil, in the northern Iraqi region of Kurdistan. Erbil was a name that leaped out at me. That was where Sam had spent the last week getting his papers in order to cross into Syria, so that was where I decided to start my search.

The phone rang a few times before a very young-sounding man answered. He introduced himself as Private First Class Something, at Security Station Point 1. I had clearly gotten through to some nineteen-year-old Marine finishing off the night shift before the consulate actually opened. "I am calling regarding my son who has gone missing in Syria," I told him.

The young man sounded very formal as I explained my surreal story. Every other word he said was "Yes, ma'am" or "No, ma'am." When I finished, he gave me a number at the State Department to call, a woman who apparently specialized in American citizens who had gone missing in Syria. It was some relief to know that such a position even existed. I thanked him and hung up.

It was very late now, after a long and stressful day. I drew some small comfort from the fact that I had actually been able to do something, so I went back to bed, resolved to call the State Department woman first thing in the morning. This time, I was able to get back into bed and actually fall asleep for a few hours.

SAM GOODWIN

Among the most striking lessons I've learned through travel is that the overwhelming majority of people in the world are well intentioned, proud of their country, and happy to help others. I could write numerous books about the positivity I experienced in all corners of the world and the utter kindness and generosity of the human species. But here I am instead, writing one book about the isolated instance in which a small subset of people hijacked the entire narrative and gave a much larger group—in this case, virtually *everyone* else in the world—a bad reputation. I don't like this narrative, and I don't like the way that only bad or negative things tend to sell in our society today. I've never enjoyed sharing negativity, especially because I've truly experienced very little of it anywhere in the world. One of the reasons I put so much time into my travel blog was to share the beauty and positivity of lesser-known and negatively perceived places. Western media often tell us there are many places we're not supposed to like, but these are the very same places in which I had many of my best, most memorable, and most positive experiences.

Unfortunately, on the night of May 25, 2019, as I was forced into my first-ever prison cell, the foundation of an unusually negative and challenging time was in place. Frankly, I didn't even know for certain that I *had* been captured. Clearly, something had gone terribly wrong—here I was in a prison cell in rural Syria—but I still didn't know why, and none of my captors seemed willing or able to explain it to me. As the metal door slammed shut, I looked around at my grim new surroundings—a windowless concrete room that I soon discovered measured exactly four steps by ten, with bullet holes gouged into the wall. The guards placed a flashlight on a shelf outside the cell door and pointed the narrow strip of light in my direction, creating a dimly lit prison cell setting similar to ones I had seen in horror movies. There were some bloodstains on the walls and a bare floor with just a blanket that was stained and crusted with who knows what bodily fluids.

Even then, I was still hoping that this had all been some misunderstanding, that these were Kurdish soldiers and there had been some snafu that would soon be resolved. The soldiers had grabbed me by the arms and pulled me out of the van, then marched me over to a building and put me in this tiny cell. Then, nothing. Nothing but me left alone to torment myself with questions and doubt. I tried to convince myself that these captors, whoever they were, had the wrong person and would soon figure out that I was not who they were after.

After a while, the door opened again. The guard gave me a plate with some boiled potatoes and a flat piece of bread that looked a bit like a tortilla. When I told the guard that I needed the toilet, he just pointed at the corner. But there was no toilet there. Clearly, they wanted me to live like a pig in a sty. When the door was closed, I peed in the corner, trying to keep the urine in as small an area as possible. Later, I really needed to poop and called for the guard again. Once more, he just pointed at the corner. But there was no way I was going to defecate in the space I had to live in. I had no idea how long I was going to be there. Thankfully, I had not eaten one of the pieces of flatbread when I had the potatoes. I carefully squatted over the bread, and when I was done, I rolled it into a shit sandwich and squeezed it through a small crevice in the wall. It felt like a small victory.

The first hours of captivity are a painful transition from the old, normal you to a new, untested person. I was facing an ordeal entirely alone, surrounded by people whose language I did not understand

and for some crime I didn't even know existed. I felt like I had committed suicide, like I had been removed from the earth, yet here I was, somehow still alive.

When I was growing up, I used to play video games with my brothers, and now, in this disorienting setting, I had the overpowering urge to hit the reset button, like my life was a game of *Mario Kart* and I had been forced by another player to crash off a cliff. Maybe I could just do that last bit again, make it right. In that cell, I also kept on half expecting Ashton Kutcher to swing open the door and yell, "You got punk'd!" It was as though all my old life references were being burned off as I hurtled into the strange atmosphere of this new world, a world in which I'd just been forced to shit on a piece of bread because there was no toilet.

I could easily understand why people break down in such situations. No doubt my abrupt isolation was partly intended to contribute to that process. After a while, though, I realized there was nothing I could do but wait. Since I'd been raised in a devoutly Catholic family, the prospect of absolute helplessness brought to mind an old expression that became a well-known country song, "Jesus, Take the Wheel." Sitting on the floor of my cell, I repeated the phrase again and again. And when the panic rose in me, I'd remind myself that this was all a misunderstanding that would get straightened out sooner or later. Eventually, exhausted, I lay down and whispered prayers to myself before falling asleep on my soiled blanket.

I slept surprisingly well that night—the weather was warm and the summer heat had not yet set in—but when I opened my eyes I realized I was still lying on the floor of a prison cell. I didn't know what time it was when the guards came in and deposited more unappetizing potatoes, which I ate anyway to keep my strength up. Then I sat, all that Sunday of Memorial Day weekend, knowing that my family was probably out on the lake in Michigan or saying good-bye to the wedding guests and heading home. I wondered what they were thinking and felt a looming terror and guilt about what they would have to undergo if I didn't get out of here soon.

But there was no sign of movement until the evening. It must have been about five o'clock when the guards came in. They told me in broken English to move.

"Where?" I dared ask.

"Erbil," said one of them who understood a tiny bit of English.

Now, that was great news, if true. Part of me—a very big part—wanted to believe them, that the bureaucratic glitch had been smoothed over. They took me outside into the courtyard and shoved me into the back of a van; then a group of soldiers climbed in next to me, filling the vehicle. It seemed we were driving back toward Qamishli. I allowed myself to hope that they'd realized I was a nobody and were sending me back to Iraq.

But then the driver pulled over onto the side of the desert road. He briefly made eye contact with the officer in charge and then pulled a blindfold out of his pocket and wrapped it around my eyes. That was when I realized I was *not* going home. The van started up again, but barely a minute later it stopped. There was a brief pause, a window opening, and I assumed we must have been going through a check-point. The vehicle moved forward, again only for a minute, then pulled up to a final halt. The doors slid open and I was pulled out of the vehi-cle. The officer took off my blindfold. In the gloomy light, I sensed there was something massive above us. I dared to glance up and realized we were standing under an enormous gray aircraft. We had pulled up right underneath it, on the tarmac of what appeared to be an airport.

One of the soldiers handcuffed my hands behind my back and I was bundled up a ladder into the cargo hold, then up again to a lower control room of the plane. They squeezed me into a small seat in what seemed like a crevice. There was some luggage that was loaded into the space in front of me—not mine—and a kid who looked to still be in his teens was left to watch me, his face serious and impassive. After about thirty minutes, an older guy in civilian clothes came and sat next to me as I clung to the last tattered shred of hope that we might be heading for Erbil.

We soon took off. It is a strange feeling to be on a plane and not know where it is going. It only reinforced that sense of powerlessness in me. As a coping strategy, I tried to cheer myself up with some humor—the only thing I knew for sure at this point was that I wasn't going to get any frequent flier miles for this flight. It barely lifted my sense of dread, so I told myself instead to focus on controlling the things I could control, speak clearly if questioned, tell the truth, and try to remain composed.

It was getting dark outside now and impossible to tell which direction we were flying or how long we were in the air. My guess was that it was around an hour and a half. North was Turkey, east was Iraq and the safe haven of Erbil. Any other direction was all Syria.

I had no idea how long we would be flying, and with all the tension, I soon found I had to pee again. My escort understood enough to hand me a bottle and then handcuff me in front of my body. I shifted my body away from him as much as I could and managed to pee into the bottle.

When we landed, I still didn't know where I was. It was clearly an airport, but I couldn't see any signs in any language. I was led down the ladder again and into a white sedan. My escort from the plane got in beside me and blindfolded me as we drove out of the airfield. Just before he covered my eyes, I managed to turn for a second and glimpse at the aircraft in full. It was huge and very distinctive. I was later able to identify it as an Ilyushin Il-76, a huge Russian military workhorse sold to Moscow's allies over the years. There were lots of people getting off after I'd been offloaded, walking down the loading ramp at the back. They all looked like civilians.

Once we were out of the airport and on the highway, the official sitting next to me took off my blindfold. After a few minutes of speeding through the darkness, I spotted a big road sign by the highway. It was in Arabic and English, and as we got closer, my heart sank. It said Damascus, with an arrow pointing straight ahead down the road we were speeding on. For many years, I had been wanting to visit Damascus, the world's oldest continuously inhabited capital and among the most religiously and culturally significant places on earth. Of course, I could have never expected my visit to happen in this way.

My hunch was that having been flown to Damascus was not good, but I tried to comfort myself as best I could. I thought about the street in the old city called Straight Street, where Saint Paul had undergone his conversion to Christianity. My revelation was that I was finally going to make it to Damascus; however, I might also not be going anywhere ever again.

Right after we passed the sign, the blindfold went back on, a little like the story of Saint Paul, who I recalled was blinded for three days after his vision of Jesus and had to be led into the city. We drove for another twenty minutes or so before we stopped and got out of the car. I was guided over steps and curbs. There was a tiny wedge of light out of the bottom of the blindfold where I could just see the floor. We walked down some stairs, and when my escort took the blindfold off, I opened my eyes to discover that I was in the dungeon of a facility I later learned is called Syria's Military Intelligence Branch 215, a prison notoriously known for housing political prisoners. It smelled like urine, like a back alley behind a row of nightclubs and bars.

A uniformed officer who spoke some English patted me down. He did a full cavity inspection, which meant squatting down so he could check my anus, another unpleasant first for me. They took my shoelaces, evidently so I wouldn't be able to hang myself, and then I was led to a cell in the back of the filthy dungeon.

The guard spoke to me in broken English. "Food. Water. Toilet. Knock," making a knocking motion against the inside of the cell door. "Otherwise, no talking." Then he slammed the door and left.

STEPHANIE (STEPH) GOODWIN,

25, Sam's younger sister

No one openly acted worried when Sam's phone call dropped that weekend of the wedding. I was sitting in the back of the van as we drove to the hotel from Ann Arbor, listening on speakerphone. I just rolled my eyes a bit because at that point, a lot of us were basically done with Sam's travels and ready for him to finish and move on with his life. I wasn't following too closely and was never quite sure where he was those days. With so many countries that I knew very little about, it became a bit of a blur.

Sam and I were very close, though. When I graduated college in 2016, Sam got me an internship with his company in Singapore. I stayed with him for about six months in Asia, and of course we hung out a lot. We're both fitness nuts, so we'd go for long runs together or work out and then eat at a popular place called SaladStop! I'd crash at his place, or he'd arrange for me to room with some of his many friends out there, including his Canadian friend Rob Martini, whom I got to know pretty well. Sam had a 200cc motorbike that we used to get around Singapore. We also went traveling throughout Southeast Asia. I knew this was my chance to have some fun and see the world before going back to the United States and finding a job, so Sam showed me some of his favorite spots. We went to the Philippines together, which was beautiful, and I did some solo traveling to Vietnam and Cambodia when he was busy at work. He knew the region and countries really well, so he helped me plan my trips.

It was a great time, and I could understand how the travel bug had bitten Sam, even though I was in Asia before he'd begun his methodical odyssey to visit every country in the world. That said, some of the places he'd been to sounded pretty unpleasant. The idea of going to North Korea did not appeal to me in the least. After six months of being based in Singapore, I couldn't wait to get home and find a job—I sell real estate in Nashville—and start a family of my own. I know Sam is a very different person, though, and any kind of office job would be anathema to him. He has a very restless, curious mind. So when he called that day from Syria, I think we were all kind of hoping he'd get over the whole travel thing soon.

The wedding was a blast, with lots of dancing and catching up with old friends. I don't think anyone was really thinking about that dropped call. The day after was Sunday, and the sister of the bride invited my sister, Betty, my brother David, and me to their family's lake house in Michigan. Mom and Dad were heading back to St. Louis, and my other brother, Paul, had to get back to New York City, as he had a busy workweek ahead. It was beautiful down by the water, and we swam and chilled out in the garden for a bit, enjoying the long weekend.

It wasn't until the following day, which was Memorial Day, that I began to get an inkling that something might not be quite right. As we were having lunch on the boat, out on the water, since it was such a pretty day, I got a text from my mom. It was on the family group chat, dubbed FAMJAM, and was asking if any of us had heard anything from Sam yet. I asked Betty and David, whose phones had pinged at the same time. They shook their heads. Then a message popped up from Paul, back in New York City. He hadn't heard anything either. We all read his message, and I remember being on that boat and the sun was shining and it was a beautiful day, but I knew at that moment that this was going to be an issue. Sam was always so good about checking in with us, and I just had a really bad feeling all of a sudden. I looked around me and it all went kind of silent, and I remember not talking about it, just wondering if the others were also as worried, or if it was just me overreacting. We finished our lunch, though I couldn't eat anything because I now had a pit in my stomach. The mood had shifted.

Later that afternoon, David drove me to the airport to catch a flight back to Nashville. I felt I had to say something.

"Hey, are you worried about Sam? Because I have a really bad feeling."

David shook his head. "No, it's going to be fine," he said, very stoic. I didn't believe him. I don't think he even believed it himself, or he was just trying to comfort his younger sister.

Right after my plane landed in Nashville, my phone rang. It was Mom again. She sounded very worried. "If I don't hear from him overnight, then we need to think about what we're going to do," she said. I agreed, though I had no idea what we would actually do in that case. I'm not sure Mom did either.

The next morning was Tuesday, and I was up at six for a workout before an early morning house-showing at eight. I was drinking my smoothie when Mom rang again. Mom was now in an intense problem-solving mode. "I don't know where he is—he didn't make it out on his flight out of Iraq," she said.

She asked me to call Rob Martini, Sam's best buddy and confidant. Sam had always shared the details of his travel itineraries with Rob. I said I'd call him, since I knew him pretty well from our Singapore days. Then Mom asked me if I remembered the name of the British singer who'd helped Sam with his Syria travel plans. Joss Stone, I recalled. She was pretty famous and had won a Grammy for her jazz and blues album. I said I'd dig out her details and contact her.

THE ROAD TO DAMASCUS

I felt sick to my stomach after that call. I couldn't even finish my smoothie. But I had a property to show, so I showered and got dressed and rushed through the viewing as quickly as I could, all the time on autopilot. Fortunately, the prospective buyers were people I knew quite well, so they didn't remark on how distracted I was acting.

As soon as I got out of the house, I jumped in my car and looked up Joss Stone on Instagram. She was pretty easy to find.

Hey Joss—this is Stephanie, Sam Goodwin's sister. We heard that you helped Sam get travel documentation for Syria and we are concerned because no one from our family has heard from him since Saturday. Would there be any way you could give us the name and contact info for the person who helped Sam cross the Iraq-Syria border? Or anyone else that may have some info about where he is??

Please email or call us any time!!

I added Mom's phone and email at the end. I had no idea whether Joss Stone even read her messages on Instagram. She was an internationally famous rock star, after all, but Sam had spoken very warmly of her.

Then I called Rob. No answer. I knew he'd be in the office already—he works in finance in Toronto—but I couldn't wait. I tried again. Nothing. Five minutes later, he called back.

No "hello," no niceties. As soon as I had him on the line, I blurted out, "Where's Sam?"

ROB MARTINI, *30, Sam's close friend*

The second I saw Steph's name appear on my phone screen, I knew something was wrong.

I'd talked to Sam on Saturday morning, when he had just checked in to his hotel. He was excited and buoyant to be in Qamishli. Interestingly though, we didn't really talk much about Syria. Sam and I have been friends for over a decade. We met in the fall of 2008 at Niagara University in upstate New York where we were both incoming freshmen on the Division I hockey team. We enjoyed our time as student-athletes, although Sam's serious concussions meant he didn't get to play much of our senior year. That did, however, give him a head start on job hunting and eventually landed him a gig in Singapore.

The NCAA level was also the end of my formal hockey career, and in early 2013, Sam called from Singapore and said he'd just joined a new start-up that needed a head of finance ASAP. I was twenty-four, still sorting out my initial professional moves and looking for new experiences. I ended up interviewing with Sam's company, accepting the job, and spending the next five years living and working in Singapore. It was a fantastic experience, especially because Sam and I were together in Asia. While based overseas, we went on some memorable trips, including taking a team of goodwill ambassadors to North Korea to coach and play against their national hockey team, and helping design an outdoor ice rink in the mountains of northern Pakistan. When I got married in 2014, Sam was my best man. Essentially, Sam is the brother I never had.

By 2019, however, I had moved back to Toronto. I was starting a new job and buying a house, and my wife was pregnant with our first child. *That* was what Sam and I mostly talked about for an hour when he called from Syria, not the backwater desert town he was visiting for a few days. But after he and I spoke on the phone that day, I was so busy with everything else going on in my life that I didn't notice on Monday that he hadn't gotten in touch with me when he was supposed to be out of Syria and back in Iraq. So when Steph's name came up on my phone, it was like a bucket of cold water had been dumped on me. I know Steph well. She crashed at my place in Singapore and invited me to her wedding, but she would almost never just call me. I nodded my way through the rest of the morning meeting with my boss and, as soon as I could, called her back.

Steph sounded deeply worried. There was no beating around the bush. I told her I had spoken to Sam on Saturday and that he sounded fine to me. Because of the time difference between Syria and the United States and Canada, we weren't initially sure if I had spoken to Sam before or after the dropped phone call with his mom in the van. Either way, no one had heard from him for three days and there was no indication he had ever gotten out of Syria.

When Sam was in Qamishli, he had sent me all the contact details for the trip. Even though Sam adventurously traveled to off-the-beaten-path places like Syria, he was always meticulous in his safety planning. I called Simon, the man who had helped Sam set up the trip. He seemed to have almost been expecting my call. The only contact he had in common with Sam was Joss Stone, and he hadn't been able to reach her. Although Simon had organized the journey, it was a friend of his who had actually been scheduled to meet Sam in Qamishli and serve as his guide. Simon knew Sam had been dropped off at the hotel, and his friend in Qamishli had eventually gone to the Asia Hotel when Sam didn't show up at the restaurant for their rendezvous. The hotel had told Simon that Sam had checked in and that as far as they knew, his bags were still in his room. They had gone and knocked on the door, and when he didn't answer, they eventually looked inside. There was no sign of Sam.

"But the town is under Kurdish control, right?" I asked Simon. "There was nothing that could have happened to him?"

It was at this point when Simon told me that not *all* of Qamishli was under Kurdish control. A very small section was still held by the Syrian regime. Assad's forces were in control of the airport on the edge of town and also small, arbitrary pockets of the downtown area. One of these spots in the city, known colloquially as the "Bermuda Triangle," is a pocket in which people have been known to simply vanish without a trace. Simon explained that even to locals, the landscape of Qamishli can be confusing and precarious.

This was when I realized we had a serious problem on our hands. I went back to my boss at work and said I had a family situation I needed to address. Then I started making phone calls.

PART II

STRANGLED BY SILENCE

SAM GOODWIN

Throughout my travels, I found some of the best hospitality anywhere in the world to be across the Middle East. In 2015, I hitchhiked the length of Oman, relying on the kindness of strangers who generously drove me from one place to the next while offering me tea and dates along the way. In Jordan, I think I ate three meals in my first hour in the country, all provided to me by my guide and his friends. In the Panjshir Valley of Afghanistan, a local man let two friends and me stay the night at his home in the mountains. The list is endless. I sometimes say that you haven't lived until you've experienced Middle Eastern hospitality.

All of these past experiences raced through my mind as I sat trapped in this Syrian dungeon. The countries of the Middle East, every one I had visited, are known for being welcoming and accommodating. So how could they be treating a "guest" this poorly? My current situation was entirely contradictory to everything else I had experienced in the region, and this disorientation ate at me.

All I knew was that I was in a dungeon. I had been frog-marched into a basement, where my handcuffs and blindfold were removed and I was put in a small L-shaped cell. There were no windows, just one light bulb on the ceiling that never went off. There were markings scratched into the concrete walls, all of them in Arabic, most likely names etched to leave some trace of the people who had passed through here. When I went up to inspect them more closely, I realized that many were crude calendars marking off the days and months of my predecessors' painful lives.

The guards didn't give me a prison uniform. I was still in the black Lululemon pants and gray T-shirt I'd been wearing when kidnapped. I would wear this exact outfit for the next four weeks in solitary confinement. Even the guards didn't wear uniforms—just jeans, sneakers, and T-shirts. They all looked pretty young too, in their early twenties, as if they were all in training. At this point there was no hint to me that I was in one of the most notorious prisons in Syria.

There were a couple of blankets and a small red washcloth on the floor. That was it, the sum of my worldly possessions. I was clearly in solitary confinement. A wave of crushing abandonment swept over me, a feeling of being completely alone in the world and forgotten. But another feeling quickly set in—the disorientation of not being able to open the door myself and just walk out. I'd been in prisons before, but only as a tourist, like Alcatraz in San Francisco and Kilmainham Gaol in Dublin. It seemed almost impossible to comprehend that I was no longer a free human being and I had no idea what was going to happen to me now.

It is rare in this modern world of endless distractions to contemplate having absolutely nothing to do, even for an hour. We are constantly on our phones, meeting people, watching TV shows, following news, reading, and moving. The need to keep up is constant. We must always be absorbing and processing new information and entertainment. All of that was suddenly gone, ripped away from me. I paced for hours those first few days, stopping only to try to interpret the calendars on the wall. I wondered at first how the other prisoners had managed to write on the walls, since I had no pen or pencil. Looking more closely, I saw that the markings had most likely been scratched into the walls with tiny pieces of cement the inmates had pried free with their fingernails. Observing the scratches and attempting to make sense of the Arabic calligraphy, I concluded that some of my predecessors had been in this tiny room for many months.

What had happened to them? I tried not to let my mind dwell on that. But in the hours and days ahead, I would hear—faint at first, then louder later on—the screams that hinted at what was really going on down here, somewhere below street level in the bowels of Damascus.

The first few days in that L-shaped cell blurred together. With the light constantly on, and no window to show me whether it was day or night, I discovered that I was going to have to figure out a way to keep track of time, like a blind person might. Twice a day, the guards would open the door to deliver food. One meal was a boiled egg with some dry flatbread, and the next meal—many hours later—was boiled potatoes and bread, very occasionally with some beans or, if I was lucky, a chunk of cucumber. Since one of the meals was an egg, it led me to assume that it might constitute breakfast and that this might be the morning.

To use the toilet, I had to bang on the metal door. My cell was in the back of the basement complex, whose exact size I couldn't determine. But the fact that it often took time for the guards to respond—and sometimes they didn't respond at all—made me think the place was pretty big and that they were busy with other prisoners. Quite often I would have to bang on the door until my hand ached. When they failed to respond to my insistent knocking, desperation led me to pee in the far niche of the cell, at the end of the arm of the L shape.

The guards had put the two cheap blankets on the floor in front of the cell door, so that is where I eventually bedded down. I folded one blanket in half to make a mattress of sorts, and I shaped the other as a cover, with one end doubling as a thin pillow.

The guards were not at all what I would have expected from an underground prison in a police state. They all appeared to be Damascus street kids. Perhaps the fact that almost all of them were so skinny made them look younger. None of them had a uniform, just casual clothes they might have worn on the streets. They looked like summer interns for the secret service. I came to think of them as the "minions." They were neither friendly nor mean. There must have been thirty of them that I saw, and among them they seemed to have a collective English vocabulary of about five words, most of which had been used up in that first conversation explaining the ground rules. If they felt like addressing me during the few seconds when they opened the door to slide in my latest meal, they would simply say, "Samwell," a pidginized Arabic version of my name, Samuel. It was to become my unofficial moniker in all my dealings with Syrian state officials. Samwell.

When the guards could be bothered to let me out to use the bathroom, I was escorted a few paces down the corridor to a hole in the floor that was slightly recessed from the hallway. A small divide half screened it from the walkway. Two of the guards would stand and watch me as I squatted down. It was humiliating at first, but there was nothing I could do about it. At least I could appreciate the moment when that awful metal door swung open and I could step out of my cell for a minute or two.

I soon discovered another huge advantage of the toilet. When I looked up, I could see a tiny window, smudged and thick with cobwebs, but with enough of a view of the sky outside to let me know if it was day or night. After this discovery, I started trying to time my toilet requests with when I thought day might be turning to night, or vice versa, just to see if I was able to track the days. Most of the time, I was relieved to see I was right. On the occasions when I'd look up and be confronted with bright daylight when I was expecting pitch darkness, it was deeply disconcerting.

I didn't speak Arabic, but I'd picked up a few words from my travels in other Middle Eastern countries. I couldn't hope to understand what the guards were saying as they stood there beside me while I squatted over the fetid hole in the corridor. But to my alarm, there was one word that seemed to surface again and again in their conversation as they glanced at me: "Daesh."

I didn't need to speak Arabic to recognize the word. Anyone who occasionally follows the news about the Middle East knows that *Daesh* is the Arabic name for ISIS, or the Islamic State of Iraq and Syria, the notorious terrorist organization known for its brutal acts of violence and its pursuit of establishing a caliphate in the Middle East. Emerging in the early 2000s, ISIS gained global attention for its ruthless tactics, including beheadings, mass executions, and the use of social media for propaganda. The group exploited political instability in Iraq and Syria, aiming to impose its extreme interpretation of Islamic law. Its territorial control peaked in 2014, but concerted international efforts have significantly weakened the organization. Despite territorial losses, ISIS remains a security threat, inspiring and coordinating terrorist activities worldwide.

Now, my guards appeared to think I was somehow connected to this group. I decided I had to change their minds quickly, for my own well-being.

I knew from my initial interrogation that my reasons for being in Syria in the first place sounded unconventional, and that had been with someone who spoke a bit of English and had access to my blog, if he had cared to check. How to let these men—on whom my day-to-day existence now depended—know why I had come here and that I was a tourist, not a terrorist?

I paced my cell, thinking, for hours. There was literally nothing else to do but focus on this. Then I saw that I had a piece of bread left over from my last meal. Slowly, carefully, I began to rip it up into miniature pieces. Then I folded the red washcloth the guards had given me and positioned it on the floor so that it would be facing the door when they opened it. Working with great deliberation and feeling like a fourth grader working on an art project, I arranged the pieces of bread to spell out the name of my Instagram handle and travel blog, @Searching4Sam. It took me hours to get it right, to make it clear enough that a non-native speaker might be able to recognize the spelling. Then I sat back and waited for the door to swing open.

When it did open the next morning, and two minions came in to take me to the bathroom, I pointed to my art project and said, "Look."

They looked at my strange creation; I said, "Instagram," repeating the word as clearly as I could several times. The word seemed to register. The guards nodded and looked again. I had spelled it out on the red washcloth because the bread was pretty much the same color as the dirty concrete floor and they might not have noticed it.

The next day, at my next bathroom break, two guards came in and pointed to the washcloth logo. One of them made a gesture like he was taking a photograph and said, "*Tamam, tamam*," or "Good, good." They smiled, then left. I never heard them say the word *Daesh* again and believe they actually did look at my Instagram.

It was a small victory, but I was soon to learn that small victories are what prison time is built on. It gave me some hope in those first few days that my message would get out to the world. Alas, at this point, I had no idea just how low my guards were in the pecking order and how little influence they had over my fate. That would only become clear in the weeks ahead.

ANN GOODWIN

At exactly eight thirty the next morning, I called the number at the State Department I had been given just a few hours earlier by the young Marine on the night watch in Iraq. It was apparently for a woman named Sara, but it went straight to voicemail. Too early, I told myself. I left a few more messages over the course of the morning, desperately but unsuccessfully trying to make contact with someone in the US government.

We didn't wait for TAG's noon deadline. No one in the family had heard from Sam, so I asked Steph to call Rob Martini. Having decided to take action, TAG immediately started working the phones, talking with Rob to find out what more he knew, as well as with Steph to start building out a potential network of contacts. Interestingly, Rob said that his sister had a college friend whose sister now worked with a guy named Luke Hartig in Washington, DC, who used to work for the National Security Council covering hostage affairs. That sure sounded like a promising lead, so TAG asked Rob to get his sister on it.

That afternoon, TAG called the FBI in their St. Louis field office. They immediately picked up and appeared to take our report very seriously. Within a couple of hours, they informed us they were sending an FBI agent from DC to St. Louis to join a team of three local FBI agents the very next morning. We were instructed to meet them at TAG's office at ten o'clock.

It was the last day of the semester at my school. The students had already completed their final exams and were out for the summer. As head of the school, I was grateful to be plenty busy, as this kept my mind from spiraling into the potential details of Sam's disappearance. Every year, we host a faculty appreciation luncheon. It ended at about two o'clock. One of my good friends on staff had broken her arm and was unable to attend. As a result, I dropped off lunch and checked in with her at her home before heading back to my house, knowing that once I was home I would have nothing to distract me. TAG was still at his office, talking on the phone. I didn't want to interrupt him by asking him how it was going. He was too busy to give me a recap.

Later that evening, my daughter Betty got home from the lake house get-together in Michigan. She and I were sitting in the family room, talking about Sam, when Steph called from Nashville. We chatted for a few minutes and then decided to say a prayer together. Betty and I sat side by side on the couch and put my phone between us, on speakerphone, so that Steph could participate as well.

We're Catholic, so we tend to recite rote prayers in our family—the Our Father, the Hail Mary, and the Rosary. The prayers are repetitive, and everyone knows what they're going to say. But I was inspired when Steph began praying spontaneously from her heart. She asked God to bring Sam home, but then she acknowledged that Sam might not come back. It was the first time anyone had said out loud what we were all privately thinking.

"Lots of people go through rough times," Steph said. "But we've had a very blessed life and we're very grateful for having Sam in our lives for thirty years. We really hope he'll always be in our lives, but we're going to accept God's will and be grateful for the thirty years we've had."

She also struck a hopeful note. "God's got this," she said. "We've always said that we fully rely on God, but we've never had to put that to the test. Right now, we need to."

I was deeply moved by that. "Wow," I said softly. "That was beautiful."

"What do you mean, 'Wow,' Mom?" Steph exclaimed. "*You* taught us this!"

That touched me even more, that my kids had absorbed the lessons I taught them, lessons of gratitude and wonder in the world around us, despite all the suffering that goes on.

That prayer reminded me of one of my most treasured moments as a family. It was back in 2007 when we traveled together on a summer vacation to Switzerland to go canyoning in a town called Interlaken. It was a perfect trip. We were all together as a family and it was during a time—individually, and as a society—before people were constantly looking at social media on their cell phones and iPads. We were just all fully present with one another, in the spectacular mountains, and I selfishly had my kids all to myself. Now, some people see God in churches, and I do too, but as I looked around at the majestic mountains of the Swiss Alps, I reminisced on the fact that I had all my kids with me, and we were all safe, happy, healthy, and grateful. I thought, "Yes, this is the Divine. The Divine is right here."

Having the people I loved the most, and all of them at the same time, in that space made it an incredibly special moment that I knew, even then, I would cherish forever. That was the moment my daughter's prayer took me back to.

ROB MARTINI

Within two hours of speaking to Steph, I had Joss Stone on the phone. She was still on her world tour, playing small gigs in every country, driven by the same urge that had led Sam to Syria. Initially, it was challenging to get through to her on the number Simon gave me, and the connection was poor when I finally made contact. I learned that the reason for this was that she was in Afghanistan, preparing to play a concert there.

I haven't had much cause to interact with musical superstars in my life, and I knew that Joss was a huge name in the industry. She'd been hailed as the "white Aretha Franklin" and had been, for a while, in a band with Rolling Stones frontman Mick Jagger and Eurythmics star Dave Stewart, but that day she just sounded like a caring and concerned friend of a fellow traveler.

I think the news came as a shock to her. She immediately offered to do whatever she could to help. Fortunately, she was traveling at that time with Paul Conroy, like she had been in Syria. Paul was a treasure trove of contacts for the region. A down-to-earth Liverpudlian, he gave me the names and phone numbers for a handful of journalists, diplomats, and officials covering Syria. I immediately phoned TAG and together we started working our way through the list, building up a picture of where Sam had gone missing and who might have a lead on more details. Most of these journalists were familiar with this region of Syria and suggested local contacts who might have seen what happened to Sam.

It's a funny thing—you hear a lot these days, when there is so much anger and instability in the world, about how grumpy or unhelpful or selfish people can be. But when we really needed help, I found it incredible how many people were willing to just spring into action. That day, and in the days that followed, I spoke to journalists from the *New York Times*, the BBC, the *Times* of London, and many more, all of whom understood the sensitivity of situations like ours and offered whatever help they could. I'd always imagined journalists, and war reporters in particular, to be hard-nosed operators only interested in chasing the story they were working on. But some of them, like Josie Ensor from the *Telegraph*, were among the most compassionate people I had ever met. They were ready to take my calls and my sometimes ridiculous questions at any time of the day or night to help someone they didn't even know. On top of this, even though this was a pretty juicy story for them—an American disappearing inside Syria—all of them kept it quiet from their editors.

In the days to come, we also learned that Liz Sly, the Beirut bureau chief for the *Washington Post*, and her photographer, Alice Martins, had entered northeast Syria on May 25, 2019, the same day as Sam. They also came via the Faysh Khabur border crossing and also checked in to the Asia Hotel, only a few hours after Sam. According to Liz, on Tuesday, May 28, members of the Kurdish military came to the Asia Hotel and told all foreigners to evacuate because a Westerner had recently been abducted from the property. Liz, Ali, and their crew immediately left Qamishli and traveled east to Derik, the same town where Joss had played her concert in February, and based themselves there for the duration of their weeklong stay in Syria. Turns out, this Westerner was Sam, and initially there was clearly some confusion among local Kurdish authorities about where he had been taken. Liz indicated that it wasn't until days later that they figured out Sam was actually kidnapped at the roundabout and not from the hotel. This insight didn't get us any closer to finding Sam, but tidbits of information like this all became part of our increasingly convoluted puzzle.

On those first few days, I worked late into the evening. When the

Middle East slipped into the night, I began mobilizing my contacts in Asia, the people Sam and I had come to know through hockey—diplomats, NGO workers, people with any business ties to the region. I couldn't explain the full situation to most of them because TAG had said we needed to keep the news on the down-low for now, but nevertheless, they promised to reach out and put me in touch with people who might be able to help. At some point, I lay down, exhausted, in desperate need of at least half an hour of sleep. But I just lay there, staring at the ceiling, knowing my best friend was in danger. There was no rest for me that night.

ANN GOODWIN

We met the FBI team in TAG's office the next morning—three agents from the St. Louis bureau and one big gun from DC. We did the introductions, and then the DC agent started to ask us questions.

He was physically fit, probably in his midthirties, and I could tell from his build and bearing that he'd been in the military at some point. His name was Paul, and it turned out he'd done security for diplomats and visiting heads of state. What impressed me the most was that from the minute he started talking to us, at around ten, until we wrapped up at four, he didn't leave his seat once, not even to go to the bathroom. He was tireless. Even as TAG and I alternated getting up for a sandwich or a drink, he remained seated at the long conference table, continuing his deliberate questioning.

The downside quickly became clear, however. The questions started off innocuously enough. He asked about the family, Sam's life from his birth to now, about hockey (down to the detail that Sam is right-handed in life but shoots left in hockey), his summers studying in France, his history of concussions, and the metal retainer on the inside of his bottom teeth.

Some of the questions were obscure enough that we had to text Rob. What was the name of the guy Sam lived with in Dubai? What's his Skype username? What was his address in Singapore?

Of course, the FBI was very interested in all the events leading up to his recent travels into Syria. Paul, the lead agent, pulled up maps of Syria on his iPad and examined possible entry routes to get to Qamishli.

He then said they would like to get a sample of Sam's DNA. That is something we never want to hear as parents. It's a grim reminder that our child may already be dead and could potentially be unrecognizable by the time he is found.

TAG called Betty, who was out for a walk with a friend, and asked her to return to the house and find something that might have traces of Sam's DNA on it. The FBI recommended a toothbrush or a hairbrush. Betty hurried home and started rummaging around Sam's old room in the basement. Sam hadn't lived at home for years but still kept a few bags there for when he visited. Looking through his belongings, Betty found an old toothbrush that she thought was her brother's. But then she found his old hockey helmet. She held it up to the light. There, in the lining, were a few dark hairs. Bingo. She jumped in the car and drove over to the meeting to deliver her prize.

By the time she got there, Paul had switched tracks on his

questioning. Now he was asking us if Sam had friends in the Middle East, whether he liked guns, if he was a loner, did he spend a lot of time online, and if he had ever shown any sympathy for extremist groups like ISIS or al-Qaeda. He was methodical, to the point, and relentless. This line of questioning must have lasted for at least three hours. After a while, when we realized where this was going, I just told him straight up, "Look, our son has not been radicalized. He's not an Islamic extremist. He didn't go to Syria to join ISIS!"

I guess he had to cover all the bases, to use his detective skills and not draw any conclusions. And the real reason for Sam going to Syria did sound a little far-fetched, even to us as we repeated it to him. The agent pointed out that Sam had lived in the Far East for the past six years. Was it possible that during that absence he had changed? That we didn't know him quite as well as we once had, as we did our other children? If he wasn't lured in by a religious extremist group, could we rule out that he was working for some other government agency, perhaps the CIA? We sensed from Paul that he was beginning to view us as naive parents who were unaware of their oldest son's purpose overseas. Sam had the character of a secret agent. He is intelligent, essentially introverted but social, physically fit, and good at putting people at ease and getting information from them. Sure, that was his natural curiosity and quiet charm, but could he have used those characteristics to work for an intelligence agency? How would a parent know?

There was a moment, coming out of the meeting later that evening, when TAG and I looked at each other and asked ourselves—*could* Sam be in the CIA? Can we absolutely, one hundred percent rule it out? But no, we just couldn't believe it.

Finally, they asked us to provide some proof-of-life questions, which only Sam could possibly know the answer to, so that if anyone established contact with him, they could authenticate that the answers came from Sam and not his captors trying to deceive us. We settled on the name of the only pet we ever owned, the names he used to address his grandparents, and the name of his first-grade teacher. As the meeting wound down, we asked Paul, the DC agent, what happens next.

"This is going to be a long process," he said. "I want you to prepare yourselves." That was not what we wanted to hear, but we said nothing at that point, except to urge them to do everything they could to get our son back.

Paul said he was going to elevate the case to the Hostage Recovery Fusion Cell, or HRFC, based in DC. This is a US government interagency group based at FBI headquarters that consists of representatives from the FBI, the Pentagon, the State Department, and other government agencies. He explained that they work together to bring back Americans who have been taken hostage or wrongfully detained overseas. It sounded impressive.

But when we asked what *we* should do, Paul said we should call the local St. Louis field office every Monday at three o'clock and an agent would give us an update on what the Fusion Cell was doing. My husband and I looked at each other. What the heck? We then told the agent we were not sitting around for weeks, waiting to talk to this local agent once a week for ten minutes to hear what some folks in DC might be willing to share with us. No way.

"That's what other families do," Paul told us.

Maybe. But we're not. No way would we be sitting there, twiddling our thumbs and waiting for someone somewhere to do something. We were going to get Sam back, come hell or high water.

The agent thought about this for a moment. Then he said, "Fine, I'll see if we can get you up to DC to meet with the Fusion Cell."

SAM GOODWIN

Control what you can control—something I learned in spades through a life of competitive athletics and something I repeated to myself countless times while detained. Despite being in a Syrian prison cell, I fought to take action and control what I could. This is somewhat counterintuitive because solitary confinement, by definition, means no action. There's no movement. It's confinement, isolation. But I wanted to take action and control what I could control. Many things, perhaps the majority of things, were out of my control. I couldn't control whether the Syrians finally figured out I wasn't a spy. I couldn't control if or when I would be released. But I could control my thoughts, attitude, prayers, and exercise. I could control how much water I drank and when I went to sleep at night. I could control my routine within that cell. My goal wasn't to get rid of negative thoughts and feelings. That's unrealistic. My goal was to change the way I responded to them.

Although I drew strength from this positive outlook, as the days passed, it began to dawn on me that I wasn't going anywhere anytime soon. The Austrian psychiatrist Viktor Frankl, who spent years in Nazi concentration camps and lost most of his family to the gas chambers, said that in the camps, the first ones to die were those who thought they would be interned for only a short time. When confronted with the fact that they could be in this hell for years, they gave up and died. The next group to die were the ones who thought they would be held forever. They too lost any reason to carry on. There is a psychological fine line between accepting a harsh imprisonment and believing that freedom will never happen. This was the line I now had to walk.

Frankl also embraced Friedrich Nietzsche's famous words, "He who has a why to live can bear almost any how," a statement that summed up my situation and mindset. Endless pacing in my cell like a behaviorally disturbed zoo animal clearly wasn't going to help. I needed a plan, a way to mark the passing of time. I was completely lost geographically—I didn't know where I was, and neither did anybody in the world who mattered to me. If I was lost in time too, I would have disappeared in every way. That way led to madness. I needed to keep track of time, to see how long I had been in the cell. If I couldn't control where I was, maybe I could at least claw back some control of *when* I was.

Think of how many times in a day we glance at our watch or cell phone clock. It's a compulsive habit for most people. Measuring time is woven into the fabric of our everyday lives. For me, in that cell, it became very different. I kept track of time in two ways. The first, as I had already begun to identify, was by when food was delivered. I established that the hard-boiled egg was being served in the morning, while the other delivery, usually bread and boiled pota-toes, came in the afternoon or evening. The second method took me about a week to discover. I noticed that when standing at the "toilet," just a few steps outside my cell, I could look up and see a small win-dow to the street, which allowed me to confirm whether it was light or dark outside. Having noticed this, I became strategic with my bathroom requests, attempting to time them with when I thought there was a change from day to night so I could verify my presump-tion. Usually, this system worked. It sounds pretty bleak, but this gave me satisfaction.

My predecessors in this cell had clearly faced the same struggle. Their crude calendars dotted the walls like cave paintings. I had no pen, but I found a small crevice in the concrete and wedged my fin-gers into the gap. After a while, and splitting my fingernails, I man-aged to work a small chip of the material loose. I now had a means of etching my own calendar into the wall, and after cross-referencing the information I obtained from both the food deliveries and my bathroom visits, I made marks on my new calendar to keep track of the days.

This proved to be one of the most important things I did. Having no clear idea of how long I had been locked away was overwhelm-ingly disorienting. As well as providing some minimal sense of gen-eral control, knowing roughly what time or day it is helps maintain some psychological awareness and an ability to remain emotionally in tune.

It didn't help that whenever the guards took me to the shower—a grim little cubicle with rat turds in the corners and a leaking metal pipe that dribbled out warm water—it was always nighttime. Maybe they were trying to confuse me, or maybe they just had so many inmates that they didn't have time to take me during the day. Either way, I was immensely grateful to be able to occasionally wash.

The next thing I needed to do was establish a routine. This was key to enduring periods of doubt and uncertainty. Structure helps maintain self-discipline and self-respect, as well as a sense of purpose. Much of this awareness I attributed to a career as an athlete and six years working for a start-up company, both of which were dramatic and humbling roller-coaster rides. Staying focused and levelheaded is critical.

Since I had nothing to do, I tried to stay asleep until the guards came with my hard-boiled egg in the morning. I knew if I woke up before that, it was just more time I had to find a way to occupy. The hardest part of solitary was the moment my eyes opened in the morning. When I was asleep, I wasn't in the cell, but the second I opened my eyes it was a startling reminder that I was still in that hole. I'd see the concrete ceiling and that light bulb and it was just a huge kick in the gut to start the day. The solution was to keep my eyes shut and try to get back to sleep, since in my dreams I was free.

It may sound odd, but I actually slept relatively well on that blanket on the concrete floor of Branch 215. I was rarely physically tired, but I was emotionally exhausted from trying to process everything that had happened and might yet happen. I was sleeping something like ten hours a day—almost half the day—and was grateful that I never started to dream of prison itself. That would have been, quite literally, a nightmare.

Having been a dedicated athlete almost my entire life, establishing a routine came naturally. When playing a sport at a high level, everything is important—diet, sleep, exercise, and so on. It all goes into being successful. Athletes have an unusual ability to learn from failure and to take those lessons and use them in a positive way. There's a kind of mental toughness, an ability to perform under pressure, that helped me extract some sense of control back from my captors.

I knew my physical health was as important as my emotional well-being. The two are inextricably linked, and every athlete knows that the release of endorphins during exercise is a great way to counteract the stress hormone cortisol. So, every day after breakfast, I would run twenty-five laps in one direction around my small cell, then twenty-five in the opposite direction. I left my bedding on the ground and used it as a kind of obstacle to jump over. During my world travels, I had once run the perimeter of the tiny Pacific Island nation of Nauru—the only time I "ran around an entire country"—and this brought back happy memories of that run in the sunshine. Then I would do what's called a push-up pyramid. This is a single push-up followed by a second-long pause, then two push-ups followed by a pause, and so on up to ten and then back down to one. My session would wind up with two one-minute planks, counting the seconds off in my head.

By the standards of Division I hockey training, or even what I'd normally do on an average day, it was minimal. But I had to take into account that I wasn't getting a significant calorie intake. I had to balance the need to keep fit with the danger of overdoing it and losing serious amounts of weight. Also, I had no change of clothes or means to wash the clothes I was wearing. I didn't want to sweat too much. I took my shirt off to exercise but kept my pants on. I guess I could have run in the nude, but the idea of being naked in a jail made me feel slightly too vulnerable.

My exercise often made me think about hockey, particularly the St. Louis Blues and how they might be doing. I knew they had beaten San Jose and advanced to the Stanley Cup Final to face Boston, but that's when my world went dark. At this point, in the grand scheme of things, I frankly couldn't have cared less about a hockey team. I was much more concerned about staying alive and the well-being of my family. But for a hostage, especially in isolation, maintaining an emotional connection to the outside is exceedingly important for psychological health, and thinking about whether the Blues might be winning helped with this. I even made small etches on my cell calendar to mark the days when I believed games were being played.

After I had cooled off from exercising, and with the rest of the day looming ahead, I would launch into the next stage of my daily routine. Even though I was alone in my cell, I would imagine I was surrounded by people—friends and family—sitting around a campfire by the lake in northern Michigan, a place dear to my heart, where my family travels for vacation in the summer. With this assembly of familiar, imaginary faces around me, I would recount to them my travels around the world, the places I had visited and the things I had seen and done. This became one of my most effective ways of occupying time in solitary confinement.

I told my imaginary audience the story of running with the bulls in Pamplona and riding rugged ponies on the steppes of Mongolia, where Genghis Khan and his Golden Horde once burst onto the world stage. I told them about the time I played pond hockey on a frozen reservoir in the Indian Himalayas and when I stood at the westernmost point of continental Africa in Dakar, Senegal. I recapped walking tame cheetahs in Zambia with my sister Betty and tracking wild rhinos on foot in Swaziland, one of the most thrilling experiences of my life. I recounted the time I ran the Phnom Penh half-marathon in Cambodia and afterward dined on a plate of roasted tarantulas. I told my campfire audience about almost being swept out to sea while exploring the blowholes of Mapu'a 'a Vaea in Tonga, way out in the vast expanse of the South Pacific, and the week I spent coaching a volleyball camp in Kabul. I explained how much I had enjoyed my summer as a student studying abroad in Lille, the postindustrial French city close to the Belgian border, and another summer teaching English in the remote village of Bagamoyo in Tanzania, delighting in the kids' enthusiasm for their studies with an American. I was able to reenact the adrenaline I experienced when jumping off cliffs near the Blue Lagoon in Malta, the enchanting island city-fortress in the Mediterranean. I described in detail the thrill of flying in a hot air balloon over the pagodas of Bagan, a fifteen-hundred-year-old city of monuments and temples in Myanmar, and floating on my back in the salt water of the Dead Sea between Jordan and Israel.

I could lose myself in these campfire talks for hours, the memories flowing through, reminding me of the extraordinary journeys that had brought me to this godforsaken spot in a basement in Syria. It freed my mind from the concrete walls around me, reminding me of who I was and of all the people in far-flung places I had interacted with over the years.

According to the United Nations, there are 193 fully recognized sovereign countries in the world. In addition, there are two countries that are nonmembers of the UN—the Holy See of the Vatican, and Palestine. There are no rules, no set criteria for what constitutes "visiting" a country. For some people, it means getting off an airplane and not setting foot outside the airport. For others, it can be weeks or months spent in each place.

For me, just going to an airport didn't count. I needed to interact with the culture, to meet people and see something of interest. I didn't have unlimited time or money or contacts, but I always made sure to connect with the country in some way. In South Sudan, I was shown around Juba by one of the twenty thousand so-called Lost Boys, who fled civil war in the 1980s. In the Philippines, a country I consider one of my favorites in the world, I cofounded an NGO that led education, leadership, and sanitation projects for underresourced children in Cebu. In Turkmenistan, I coached hockey, swam in a cave, and went hiking near the Iranian border. I had a Turkish bath on the northern, Turkish-run side of the divided island of Cyprus, whose capital, Nicosia, is still bisected by a miniature version of the Berlin Wall. I rode an ATV on the sand dunes of the Sahara in eastern Morocco, gave an elephant a bath in Thailand, saw marijuana plants growing by the roadside in the Himalayan country of Bhutan, and played soccer on the beach with local kids in Liberia, a West African country originally established as a haven for former African American slaves after the US Civil War.

Of all the places I've experienced, my visit to North Korea is among the trips I get asked about the most, not least because the man who arranged it was himself to end up a hostage in a prison in China at the same time I was in a cell in Syria.

In late 2015, I got connected with Michael Spavor, a Canadian who was fluent in Korean and had lived in the Far East for years, through the regional ice hockey community in Asia. Michael was based in Dandong, on the Chinese side of the North Korean border, where he founded the Paektu Cultural Exchange, an NGO that promoted sports and cultural exchanges between the Hermit Kingdom and the rest of the world. He was well connected inside North Korea and one of the few Westerners to have actually met Kim Jong Un. In addition, it was Michael who arranged the rather surreal sports diplomacy mission by the former Chicago Bulls star Dennis Rodman to visit the basketball-obsessed Kim in 2013 a few years after the young heir had taken over from his late father.

In March 2016, when I was living and working in Singapore, Michael arranged for a group of North American and European ice hockey players to go and coach and play against the North Korean national team. Rob and I both signed up and were eager for the opportunity. But the entire trip almost got derailed even before it began. A few weeks before we were supposed to leave, the North Koreans arrested an American college student, Otto Warmbier. He had gone there on a guided tour, and as he was about to board his flight home at Pyongyang airport, he was arrested for stealing a propaganda poster from the hotel. For this trivial infraction, he was later sentenced to a shocking fifteen years of hard labor.

The arrest certainly gave us pause as we prepared to leave for Pyongyang. But in the end, we decided to go ahead, assured that we were there as part of a goodwill mission to simply reach out to and engage with ordinary North Korean people. The trip was fantastic, and we were treated like royalty. We were shown the city by smiling, friendly guides, aware that our every move was monitored. But we also got to skate with young men our own age who shared the same passion for hockey.

Even though we couldn't directly communicate with them verbally, we connected as athletes and saw one another as normal people, as opposed to ideological foes bent on mutual destruction. That is the power of travel and human connection. Aside from hockey, I probably could not have had less in common with the North Korean players given my perspective on the world and the life I've been fortunate to live. But once that puck dropped, our relationship ran like a Swiss watch. We knew exactly where to go, what to do, and how to best work together to score goals. Nobody was bothered by political discrepancies, demarcation lines, or nuclear weapons. We built a magical bond through the game of hockey, and it was a remarkable demonstration of humanity. Michael arranged a fantastic experience for us in North Korea.

Otto was returned to the United States the following June, in a vegetative state. His family believes he was tortured in jail, and US doctors who examined him disputed the official North Korean version that he was suffering from botulism and the side effects of a sleeping pill. Otto died a few days after being flown home. He was just twenty-two years old.

Should I not have gone on this trip? Did the simple human connection I made with those young North Korean players in any way outweigh the horror their government inflicted on an innocent young American? It is difficult to say. All I know is that ordinary North Korean people themselves are the first victims of the dictatorship in their country, and if my visit helped inform them, in even the slightest way, that there was a better world waiting out there—not one waiting to destroy them if their loyalty to the Kim dynasty ever wavered—then I think my visit was worthwhile.

In December 2018, Michael became a victim of international power politics. He and another Canadian, former diplomat Michael Kovrig, were arrested by Chinese authorities and held on trumped-up spying charges. Thankfully, the case of the Michaels would go on to end peacefully, but as I would later learn, at that point my friend Michael and I were both being detained in a foreign country on false charges of espionage at the same time.

Perhaps equally as precarious, in June 2019 while I was in Branch 215, Joss went on to reach the finish line of her Total World Tour, with her final country being Iran. When Joss and I chatted at the airport in Fiji in May, I suggested she and her team go to Kish Island instead of mainland Iran, as it is a visa-free haven for travelers and a place I visited several years earlier. I had a wonderful experience, celebrating New Year's Eve there, in fact. When Joss arrived on Kish in late June, she was "detained and deported," reportedly because women are not allowed to "perform" publicly in the country. Joss later explained to me that all of the Iranian officials were very kind to her and her team, but they did hold them in a hotel under close supervision for one night before forcing them to fly out the next morning. To this day, Iran remains the only country in the world in which Joss has not performed.

Despite the concept of detention looking very different for Joss and me, it's a bit paradoxical to think that I had recommended a way for her to travel to Iran and she had recommended a way for me to travel to Syria—and we both got detained as a result.

Although recapping my stories from around the world pleased my imaginary prison cell audience, I determined that some stories were best not to dwell on in my campfire talks.

TAG GOODWIN, *63, Sam's father*

It took a few days for the enormity of the situation to sink in, but when it finally did, it hit me hard.

It had seemed not unreasonable for a phone call to have dropped in Syria. When Ann was getting worried those first couple of days, I was less concerned and preferred to wait and see how the facts played out. By Tuesday night—three days after anyone had spoken to Sam—the awful reality started to really bear down on me. My eldest son was missing on the other side of the world.

I feared I might be overwhelmed by the sheer horror of it, and the thought of what loomed ahead. I knew it would be an incredible struggle. The situation was more grave and certainly more personal than the business challenges—sales, marketing, finance, operations, personnel—I'd been accustomed to resolving throughout my career.

I identified early on, though, that the playbook for success would likely be the same but on steroids—define the problem and objectives, recruit a best-in-class task force, and develop a detailed action plan and get to work executing it.

Despite this approach, I still worried about how I would physically and emotionally cope with the task ahead, but I knew I had to do so effectively if we were going to have any hope of finding Sam. I had a fairly demanding corporate job. I was senior vice president at Parsons, a multinational civil engineering company. I knew I'd have to put my work on a back burner without giving too much away to my coworkers, given that we were supposed to keep the whole thing under wraps.

Relatedly, I was also uneasy about my company's connection to the US government. Although my focus was on civil infrastructure and improving the nation's roads, bridges, and rails, other divisions of Parsons work closely with the US military and intelligence community. I worried that if Sam was in the hands of the Syrian government, Syrian officials might think I was involved in those areas, and that might make it easier for them to imagine he was somehow a spy. I was aware that there was nothing I could do about that, but it was still quite bothersome. I also knew the only way I would be able to get through all this would be to throw myself all-in to getting him out.

Earlier that day, I had already begun tracking down journalists who covered the region to see what they knew about Qamishli. I was impressed by how intentional and willing they were to go out of their way to try to help. One in particular, Jane Arraf from NPR, spent multiple hours describing to me the situation in the region and promised to put out feelers among her contacts in Syria to see if they heard any news while also agreeing to keep it all hush-hush. She even contacted the acting US ambassador to Iraq about Sam, which essentially meant that the State Department was now notified. But she still recommended we call the US Overseas Citizens Services in Washington. Turns out, this was the same office that Ann had been referred to by the Marine on the night shift in Erbil. I called the number and spoke with a guy named Thomas, whom I found to be unhelpful. He transferred me to a woman named Sara, the same woman Ann had contacted, who is a Syria country officer and evidently handles calls about missing people. Piggybacking on Ann's previous messages, I also left her a very detailed voicemail and asked her to return my call. When neither of us heard anything back, I assumed she was in touch with the Baghdad embassy and was coordinating a response with them. Boy, was I ever wrong. We soon learned she was out of town and apparently neither she nor anyone else was checking her voicemail. We heard crickets from the ambassador in Baghdad too.

In those first several days, we learned a lesson that would become central to our search and rescue operation—when dealing with government bureaucrats, *never assume anyone is doing anything.*

These channels were only the beginning. I was constantly on the phone with Rob, strategically brainstorming our next moves. Ann and all of our kids were also reaching out to whomever they thought could be of any use, no matter how remote they might be. Our son David had spent a summer working for the Catholic Church in Cuba thanks to a pastor in Florida, Father Richard Vigoa. *Give me his number and I'll call him.*

Since we were heading to DC to meet with the special hostage group, I also called Sam's good friend Ben Stephan. Ben is originally from DC and had studied with Sam in France in the summer of 2010. He was living in Utah at the time but dropped everything to fly in to help us navigate the bureaucracy of DC. Every day—every hour—the list of people to contact got longer and longer. I kept a journal of everyone I'd talked to, noting what they'd said and whom they in turn had recommended we contact. From a tiny dot of our family and friends, our network started to inch out across the world.

It had struck me that the gargantuan task of getting my son out of Syria was going to take a toll on me, both physically and emotionally. My own well-being didn't worry me so much as the fact that any illness would impinge on my ability to keep on doing what I was doing. In the evenings, as the office was shutting down, I would go to the Missouri Athletic Club, a social, athletic, and dining club where our family has been members for years, to exercise and attempt to decompress, which helped me keep fit and sleep a little better, for the few hours I was able to sleep. Afterward, I would find a quiet corner and sit down to work the phones and then write up my notes, working well into the night, slowly searching for a way to find my son.

ANN GOODWIN

The FBI advised us not to speak to anyone outside of our immediate family about Sam's case. Despite this, in mid-June, I needed a favor from my close friend Kathy. Her husband also happens to be a friend of TAG's, so I felt I could trust her with our secret.

Kathy is among the most positive people I've ever met, always smiling and beaming with energy. I've been known to turn to her for a range of things, from designing my front yard flower bed to proofreading my résumé to improving my pickleball game. Kathy has a lot of gifts.

This time, however, when I reached out, I told her I needed a dress for a funeral. I then let her in on some of the details of our family's ongoing situation and explained that some experts were suggesting that Sam was already dead. We didn't know this for sure, but in the event that this news were to prove to be true, I knew I wouldn't have the emotional bandwidth at that time to grieve with our family and shop for a dress, so I wanted to handle it now. I wasn't at all throwing in the towel or losing faith, but instead just being practical.

Kathy replied, "Wait, wait. I'm happy to go shopping for you, but let's also try to gather more information about Sam."

I thanked her, but in fact I was already praying that I'd rather Sam be peacefully in heaven than be tortured inside a Syrian prison cell on earth.

PART III

SIX DEGREES OF SEPARATION

BETTY GOODWIN, *24, Sam's youngest sister*

W hen I was asked to find something of Sam's that might have his DNA on it, the weight of the whole situation really began to sink in.

Although he'd been living and working overseas for so many years, Sam kept some of his belongings in the basement of our parents' house, where he also had a bed to sleep in when he visited home. As I grabbed his old hockey helmet, it struck me that the FBI would soon be scouring these mementos of our childhood for traces of my brother, to match the DNA with a body that may not be otherwise identifiable. It was almost too much to take in, so I stuffed them in a bag and headed over to my dad's office, where the FBI was interviewing my parents.

I was living at home in St. Louis that summer, having just finished a master's degree in higher education and administration at Boston College. In the fall, I was due to begin a year volunteering in Denver with an organization that works with the local homeless population. Until then, though, I had a few months of freedom. The highlight of my summer was to be a monthlong pilgrimage walking across northern Portugal and Spain, the famous Camino de Santi-ago. It's a beautiful hike through historic cities and stunning coun-tryside commonly known in English as the Way of Saint James. The cathedral at the end of the route is famous for being the final resting place of Saint James, one of Jesus's apostles and the brother of John. It was a major pilgrimage route in the Middle Ages. I'd seen a movie about the 365-mile trail and thought it would be a perfect oppor-tunity to explore, pray, and reflect after finishing a year of intense studying and before moving on to the next stage of my life.

I was due to fly to Portugal with a friend to start the pilgrimage just a week after that meeting with the FBI. It was a fraught week. All we could do was think about Sam, talk about Sam, pray for Sam. Even when we tried to go for a walk to take our minds off it, prom-ising each other to talk about something else, within two minutes we'd be talking about Sam again. We are a very tight-knit family, and we'd always had the sense that if we stuck together, there was nothing we couldn't beat, but this one seemed insurmountable. For the first time, we felt helpless, just when it mattered the most. I told my parents I would call off the trip, but they were insistent that I go. They wanted their kids to try to carry on with as normal a life as pos-sible. In the end, I went.

Like Sam, I love to travel, and I had joined him on some of his incredible trips. We explored southern Africa together, where we swam in Devil's Pool at Victoria Falls. We stayed in an elephant lodge in Botswana, a country that is home to more elephants than any other in the world, one of those weird facts you pick up when traveling with Sam. He was the best travel companion, always made friends wherever he went, always planned the most interesting, off-the-beaten-path places to see. He has a burning curiosity, combined with a fantastic memory for facts, so I always learned a lot on the road with him. People were always asking him for tips about holidays or places for a special honeymoon, because he literally had been everywhere. Truly, it was Sam's best qualities that had led him to Syria.

When I originally planned my trip to the Camino, I had wanted to go off the grid so I could be fully present in a retreat-like setting. Given the circumstances, though, my mom apologetically requested that I call her every day, which I agreed to do.

We set out from Fátima, the historic town where the Blessed Virgin Mary has appeared to various people over the centuries. The first reported sighting was in the middle of the eighteenth century, when she appeared to a mute shepherdess who was able to speak after the encounter. Then, in 1917, Our Lady of Fátima appeared six times to three children guarding their family's sheep. People then began flocking to the spot, which rapidly became a major pilgrimage site. Unfortunately, the Spanish influenza epidemic claimed the lives of two of the children a couple of years later, but on May 13, 2017, Pope Francis canonized them, exactly one hundred years after their first vision.

It was encouraging to be hiking a trail littered with so many miraculous stories, because it seemed my family was going to need its own miracle if we were ever going to see Sam again. Sam had told me about his visit to Fátima during his voyage, so it had an extra-special feel.

The ancient pilgrimage route led us through some spectacular big cities, like Porto, which gave its name to the fortified wine, but much of it was rural backcountry, little towns and villages travelers would never otherwise see, and olive groves and fields with the Atlantic Ocean sometimes providing a windswept backdrop off to the west.

Along the way, I made sure to light a candle and say a prayer for Sam in every church we passed, no matter how small. In some of the tiny villages we passed through, there'd be no one in sight, but the door to the ubiquitous small chapel would always be open, so I would let myself in and carry out my ritual. By the time we made it to Santiago, there must have been a hundred candles flickering in front of church altars.

The FBI had told us we shouldn't tell anyone outside of the family about Sam's disappearance, but of course I had to tell the friend I was walking with. Along the way, I bumped into a priest I'd known in Boston and told him about it too. He was traveling with a group of other priests, and he said he would get them all to say a daily prayer for Sam, which I greatly appreciated.

Walking was a great way for me to unburden myself, as was prayer. The Camino helped me get through that hard first month of knowing next to nothing about Sam. My sister, Steph, would occasionally call me in Europe to give updates on the search, but the news wasn't encouraging. Also, we had no idea if the Syrians might be bugging our phones—this was how little we knew about the Middle East—so if there was some potentially sensitive information to share, Steph would sometimes FaceTime me and hold written messages up to the screen so nobody would overhear her sharing.

Finally, we reached Santiago, a stunning old city of winding stone streets, sweeping royal plazas, and, of course, the glorious cathedral that dominates the skyline, and where a daily mass is held for the pilgrims who are always trickling in. Amid its soaring Romanesque columns, I lit my final candle of the journey and begged God to bring my brother back home to us safely.

SAM GOODWIN

Following my exercise routine and storytelling, it was time to pray. In prison, prayer is done with particular intensity, one that is compounded by solitary confinement.

My Catholic faith was a big part of my travel journey. Over the years, I had made specific efforts to visit religious sites around the world, including Fátima in Portugal, Medjugorje in Bosnia and Herzegovina, and the Basilica of the Presentation of the Blessed Virgin Mary in Wadowice, Poland, where John Paul II was baptized. I've twice enjoyed the Scavi Tour underneath St. Peter's Basilica in Rome, and the crux of my visit to Israel just a few months before landing in prison was to visit the Holy Land sites. One of the most compelling things for me about traveling to Syria was its religious significance. Mary Magdalene was of Syrian descent, King David conquered northern Syria, and the conversion of Paul the Apostle took place on the road to Damascus. I've been to Mass in 65 countries and visited Catholic churches in 115. I was planning to attend Mass on Sunday, May 26, in Qamishli, but God clearly had other ideas.

In solitary confinement, my prayers became an uninterrupted conversation with God. I was constantly talking to him while physically pacing back and forth. Even though the guards told me not to talk, I prayed out loud. *God, I'm here, I'm listening. What are you trying to tell me today? What can I learn today? What are, perhaps, the positives about my situation today?*

One thing was always at the top of my prayer list—*Please let me get out of this place physically unharmed.* Even in my distant corner of the basement dungeon, I could hear the muffled screams emanating from the prison's epicenter, and they felt like a warning of what was to come.

I didn't want to stay in isolation in Syria for years either, so the next prayer on my daily litany was about the timing of my release, assuming my first prayer was answered. I remember positioning this prayer almost like a business deal. *God, I know you have a plan, but is it possible you might consider an adjustment to the timeline? Can that work with your plan?* Not only for myself, but for my family, who I knew would be praying and suffering too.

I then finished all of my prayers by saying the Rosary. I didn't have a physical rosary, but I'd recite fifty Hail Marys while walking around the cell, divided into ten decades, just as my mother had taught us when we were kids. Each decade was dedicated to something different. I prayed for my family, my friends, and for anyone I thought might be working to get me out of this situation. If nothing else, prayers like this took my mind off of immediate fear and anguish, offering some relief.

Having seen the suffering of the world firsthand and given my current situation, I prayed for world peace. Last, I prayed hard for the courage to forgive my captors. Through this, I discovered that I was working to forgive people who weren't even sorry, which is real strength. Forgiveness is not a feeling, I came to realize. It's a choice. Although I had no indication that my captors were sorry, on the off chance that they were, my forgiveness was there, and I would bear them no resentment.

Of all the things I did to survive in prison, nothing brought me as much peace and comfort as those prayer sessions. Everything I'd ever had, or known, had been stripped from me—my means of communicating with anyone, my material possessions, my freedom. But no matter what, I knew that my faith was absolute, and I didn't need a phone or permission from the guards to talk to God. This is what I had to lean on when everything else was gone, and I know I would have been in a completely different situation without that faith, that knowledge. I truly believed that this was not the end, that I had a purpose in life and that there was more for me to do. I was going to get out of this, even if I didn't know when. This was not how things ended.

We're never less alone than when we're totally alone with God, and I was totally alone with God. In that Syrian dungeon, I felt a closeness, a connection, that I've really never felt before, and which, I have to admit, I've not felt since, in this world of cell phones, twenty-four-hour news, and hyperconnectivity.

Over the weeks, I found the fear slowly receding. Not that I ever stopped caring about dying or never seeing my family again, but I began to simply lose the energy to be afraid. Fear is an emotion, and I was so emotionally and psychologically exhausted that I began to lack the energy to generate it. In some ways it was liberating, in other ways it felt like I was dying. But even there, I found some unlikely comfort. After all, there is nothing more certain in life than death, and no one in history has managed to conquer it. So on the rare occasions when my faith flagged—and I admit it did—and I thought my prayers would never be answered, I faced the truth that I might just die here. While that was a terrifying thought, at the end of the day, at least I knew my fate would be no different than anyone else's.

FATHER RICHARD VIGOA,

49, pastor at St. Augustine's Parish, Miami

I had just gotten off a plane from Cuba, where I had been visiting Havana for the five hundredth anniversary of its founding, when my phone started pinging. There is limited cell phone service and internet in Cuba, so I had missed all of TAG's desperate calls that morning. As soon as I landed, my phone snapped to life and I saw a troubling text message.

"Father Vigoa, TAG here. I tried you but it went to voicemail. Sam has been missing in Syria since Saturday. Our State Department is engaged. Do you have any Catholic Church connections in Syria that have good communications with the Syrian government? Thank you."

There was scant detail, but what there was told me this was bad. Really bad.

By the spring of 2019, I'd known the Goodwins for several years. My first contact with them had been a few years earlier when I was talking with a friend in Miami who said he had a business associate from a Catholic family in St. Louis. The father was looking for a summer job for one of his boys. Maybe he could do some work with the church in Latin America, to improve his Spanish and see a bit of the world?

As it happens, we were always looking for volunteers and missionaries to go to Cuba, since the church there is pretty beleaguered in the middle of an atheist Communist state. In fact, before John Paul II made the first-ever papal visit to Cuba in 1998, it was actually against the law to practice any religion on the island. Even Christmas was banned.

That was how I met Sam's younger brother David, for whom I found an internship that summer helping out at the church of Santa Clara, a city in central Cuba and a diocese I've visited a few times. I am the pastor at St. Augustine Church, which serves the students of the University of Miami, but being of Cuban descent, I try to help the church there as much as possible, and I thought this would be a good fit for David and an opportunity for him to practice his Spanish. So David went off to Cuba and we quickly became close friends.

A couple of years later, when Sam set off on his travel odyssey, he and I would occasionally exchange Instagram messages. Since the Catholic Church is spread around the entire planet, I was able to occasionally help him out by introducing him to various priest friends and papal nuncios, which are Vatican ambassadors who represent the Holy See diplomatically, especially in Africa. They were happy to meet the young American. They might offer him a meal, a place to stay for a couple of nights, or some local contacts to help him on his way. Sam once told me of his surprise and delight when he got off a flight in Burkina Faso and there was a Vatican car waiting for him planeside to take him to meet the nuncio in Ouagadougou for dinner.

But by that spring weekend in 2019, I hadn't heard from the family for a few months. There were no more details in TAG's text, but clearly this was bad. I called him back right away, offering to do whatever I could to help. From that moment on, I was involved with the family daily, helping to find ways into the closed world of Syria's prison system while also attempting to offer comfort to the family through the strength of our shared faith. I didn't know anyone in the church in Syria, but I was pretty sure I could track someone down. I had worked as the priest secretary to the archbishop of Miami for nine years, and that experience helped me establish many contacts. There is almost no corner of the globe where the Catholic Church isn't active.

My first call was to Catholic Relief Services in DC. CRS is an international relief agency not unlike the Red Cross. It operates in some very unstable environments and often has to use skilled diplomacy to navigate conflicts or situations where human rights are being abused. I called one of the senior officials at CRS whom I happened to know. He gave me the cell phone number of a colleague in Lebanon but told me not to let the person know who'd given it to me. I eventually managed to connect with this guy, who in turn gave me the phone number of the nuncio, or papal envoy, to Syria, Cardinal Mario Zenari.

This was significant. Cardinal Zenari is a senior Vatican ambassador with one of the most sensitive portfolios in the world. In addition, Cardinal Zenari is close with Debra Tice, mother of Austin Tice, the American freelance journalist who went missing in Syria in 2012 and whose status remains unknown. Debra says that Cardinal Zenari was like a brother to her in the early days of Austin's captivity. Even though Syria and the wider Middle East are largely Muslim, the region is also the cradle of Christianity. Syria has one of the oldest Christian communities in the world. In fact, much of the population of Damascus received its ministry directly from Saint Peter himself, and at the time was the first and largest Christian community in the world. At least half a dozen popes were born in Syria. While the largest part of the modern Syrian Christian community is Eastern Orthodox, there is also a sizable population adhering to the Melkite Greek Catholic Church and Maronites, Armenian, and Syriac churches. Together, Christians make up around 10 percent of the Syrian population.

This all made Cardinal Zenari a crucial figure in efforts to protect the welfare of the Syrian Christians. He was also challenging to get hold of, shuttling between Damascus and Rome. The seventy-three-year-old had been appointed by Pope Benedict XVI to be the papal representative to Syria in late 2008, three years before the Arab Spring erupted across the Middle East and triggered Syria's own civil war. But if anyone could potentially get Sam's case to President Assad, I assumed it would be the cardinal.

He was in Rome when I finally managed to get him on the phone. I quickly explained Sam's story, saying that he had been trying to travel to every country in the world and explaining how he helped local communities and tried to build bridges between communities, but had vanished in Syria and now his family was trying to find him.

The cardinal immediately communicated to me the complex nature of the situation.

"Do you understand the position you are putting me in?" he asked. "Sam is probably going to die in Syria."

I tried to placate him. "I understand, Your Eminence, and I am very sorry to ask you this, but we love him and we want him to come home."

The cardinal remained reluctant. I understood—he was in one of the most delicate positions imaginable, shepherding a Christian community that had shrunk dramatically in recent years because of the violence in the region and that was still vulnerable to attack by violent extremists. It was an unenviable task, but he was in probably the best position I knew to have access to the upper echelons of the Syrian government.

I gave him my contact details, and he eventually said that he would see what he could do. A little while after our conversation, I received an email from the cardinal, which was slightly more encouraging. Part of his email is here:

Dear Fr. Richard,
I feel very sorry for Mr. Sam. For sure he will be considered a spy. I feel sorry.

I see the matter very complicated and I fear that the consequences will be grave. I know a little bit about the Syrian regime, after an experience of 10 years. The US government has

to deal with this issue. Anyhow when I shall return to Syria next
month of July (now I am in Italy). I work on this and try to have
some news.

Mons. Mario Zenari

At least he had promised to try. That was all I could realistically
ask for at that point.

Just in case the cardinal might need some encouragement, Ann,
Sam's mother, also drafted a letter to Pope Francis himself, which I
translated into the Holy Father's native Spanish.

Holy Father
We write to beg for your assistance in interceding for our son, Sam
Goodwin, who is being detained in Syria. It is our understanding
that he is being held by the Syrian regime. We need your help to
communicate to the Syrian regime that Sam is of no interest to
them. He has no military experience and no political agenda.
Our family is seeking your assistance, Holy Father, to bring our
son and brother home safely so that he may continue to be light in
a dark world. We ask that you please speak with His Eminence,
Cardinal Mario Zenari, Apostolic Nuncio in Syria, to please
help in this effort. We believe that his intervention is crucial to
bringing Sam home. We will be truly blessed by any assistance
the Church is able to offer.

I then contacted Cardinal Seán O'Malley, the archbishop of
Boston, who is a friend. He was due to meet with the pope on an

upcoming trip to Rome and agreed to personally deliver the letter. That was a great relief, but I was far from finished.

Another useful thing about the Catholic Church is that, as well as being a global faith, it is also a sovereign nation. Vatican City is tucked inside an enclave in Rome, but its status opened up a whole slew of official diplomatic channels for us to pursue. At the same time that we were starting to reach out to church leaders in Syria, I contacted the Vatican envoy to the United Nations in New York to open a diplomatic path. The papal nuncio, officially the Permanent Observer of the Holy See to the United Nations, agreed to try to set up a meeting with his Syrian counterpart.

All of these channels seemingly represented a bit of progress. In addition, I asked my entire parish, St. Augustine, in Coral Gables, Florida, to pray for Sam. I even taped a picture of Sam to the statue in our church of Saint Anthony, the patron saint of lost things.

PART IV

DIPLOMATIC DEADLOCK

ANN GOODWIN

A week after that first meeting with the FBI in St. Louis, TAG and I flew to DC to meet with the Hostage Recovery Fusion Cell. On the plane, I was filled with hope that we would now be launching the might of the US government, with all its expertise and resources, into the search for Sam.

Oh my, was I in for a shock.

TAG warned me not to get too excited. He had determined after our first encounter that they were clearly more interested in establishing that Sam was not a member of ISIS than actually doing much to get him back. Their intentions were sincere, but they seemed to be well in over their heads. This was why TAG had organized a range of other meetings in Washington for the same trip. Still, I was hopeful that since we were now meeting with the big guns in the capital, things would start looking up.

The J. Edgar Hoover Building looks like a giant concrete bunker plopped down on Pennsylvania Avenue overlooking the National Mall. At the entrance, there is an airport security–style checkpoint at which everyone must empty their pockets and walk through a metal detector. Official visitors then proceed through a series of security gates like airlocks into segmented areas that are sealed off from one another. If the security is state of the art, the decor is not. The corridors we passed through were lined with worn linoleum tile and off-white paint, a stuffy government atmosphere I had only seen on TV.

Finally, we emerged into a large interior courtyard, which was like a breath of fresh air after the 1970s style box of a building. There were walkways, picnic tables shaded by umbrellas, and a statue on the green artificial turf of three figures representing the core values of the agency—fidelity, bravery, and integrity. I looked up at the third-floor balcony and could see a group being given a guided tour. At that moment, I wished that I was part of a group of tourists being shown around the building and not someone here on official FBI business.

Paul, the agent we'd met in St. Louis, sat us down and gave us a briefing on what to expect in the meeting. He explained the various government agencies and the sorts of things they would be talking about. He was very courteous, as though we might be intimidated by the place or the people. I wasn't intimidated. I just wanted to get in there and hear what they could do for my son.

The meeting itself was in a large conference room. We learned that because this room is a "sensitive compartmented information facility," or SCIF, we had to leave our cell phones in small cubbies outside so no one could listen to our conversations. The meeting consisted of a dozen or so people sitting around a hefty boardroom table—representatives from the FBI, the CIA, the military, and the State Department, among others. They were all very pleasant and concerned, and they came up to us individually to introduce themselves while promising to do all they could to help.

In our courtyard briefing, I had asked Paul, our case officer, if the people at the Fusion Cell even knew what Sam looked like. He'd reassured me that everyone had been fully briefed, so I was relieved when I entered the conference room and saw a large screen on the wall with a picture of Sam next to a map of Syria.

Everyone took their places around the table, each one behind a paper tent labeled with their name and agency. The lead FBI agent began the meeting by asking each person to explain to us their capabilities.

The State Department representatives went first. I was quite taken aback when they said they couldn't really do much because the US government had no diplomatic relations with Syria. They explained that all official American engagement with the Assad regime was being handled by the Czech Republic, which serves as the "protecting power" for US interests in Syria. They then admitted that they didn't recommend going via this channel.

Next were the officials from the military. "We don't know where Sam is, so we can't send in the SEALs or the US special forces," they said. They did ask me, however, should they learn the location of my son, would I want to send in a rescue mission? I thought about that for a minute and then said no. "I don't think I can send in another mother's son and risk their lives to get my son. We need to find another way to get Sam out without anybody getting hurt," I said.

Ambassador Laura Dogu, who was the deputy director of the Fusion Cell, spoke next. She is sharp and knowledgeable, and she has excellent communication skills. I liked her a lot. She had previously served as the US ambassador to Nicaragua, in addition to other assignments around the world. Throughout our engagements with the Fusion Cell, Laura was my confidant. She would patiently and repeatedly answer all of my questions and educate me on the geopolitical landscape of the Middle East.

Sitting next to Laura was a woman who identified herself as the Fusion Cell's negotiator. "I will negotiate Sam's release if the Syrians reach out to the US government and want to negotiate," she said. If Sam was being used as a political chess piece by the Syrian regime, they would ask for something in return that Washington was unlikely to ever give them, something like money or advanced weapons. The US response would be to counteroffer with some form of humanitarian aid, such as a water treatment plant or a mass vaccination campaign—something to better the lives of the Syrian people. I liked this idea, that Sam's case might somehow help ordinary Syrians, but at the same time, the thought flashed through my head, "I may never get my son back," as now four people had essentially told us they couldn't really do much. I was also thinking that if Sam's captors reached out and wanted to negotiate, *I* wanted to be the one to negotiate on his behalf, not the government. I didn't voice this, though, because at the time we believed the Fusion Cell was Sam's best chance of coming home safely and didn't want to say or do anything that would demotivate them from working as hard as they could to find him.

Next up were the CIA representatives. "We don't have anyone in Syria at present, so we cannot do anything," they said. I was shocked. Surely the storied Central Intelligence Agency had agents or informants everywhere, right? In addition, Syria was such a huge issue—American special forces troops were deployed there for missions—that they must have people there, in some capacity. We strongly suspected that they were not being forthcoming with us.

Finally, it was the FBI's turn. The Fusion Cell is based at FBI headquarters, and we hoped they would have something to offer. Nope. The FBI said the situation in Syria was such that they couldn't do anything there. They did, however, offer us the services of a doctor, to provide whatever stress-relieving medications we might need, or marriage counseling, as the pressure of situations like ours had ripped marriages apart in the past.

By this point, I was feeling pretty gutted. This looked like an excessive use of time for minimal results. These people clearly meant well, but it seemed like they were going to function as a resource instead of a solution. Each member of the Fusion Cell team was seemingly smart and an expert in their respective field, but collectively they lacked coordination and were therefore ineffective for us. We didn't need a doctor or a marriage counselor. We needed them to bring Sam home, and they seemed to have forgotten that this was why we were all here in a giant concrete bunker in the first place.

"Listen," I told them, my school administrator instincts kicking in. "Let's just start over for a minute here. I'm going to ask you questions and I want you to answer me." I then randomly called on people, flitting around the table, looking at the name tags. I wanted to see if they really knew anything about Sam and his story.

"Can you tell me who Rob Martini is?" I asked one. "Can you tell me who Simon Khayat is?" I asked the next person. "Can you tell me why Sam was in Syria in the first place? Is he physically fit? Do you even know his story?"

The assembled agents and officials looked startled at being treated like students, quizzed over whether they had done their homework. To me, it just came naturally. They did all right, though, I have to admit. I was slightly reassured by the fact that they had at least read the briefing notes. But they didn't like this activity, not one bit.

The Fusion Cell then made a striking comment but in a matter-of-fact tone.

"If you want your son home, *you* are going to have to find an influencer of President Assad, someone who can plead his case," they said.

A couple of weeks before this, I hadn't even known exactly who President Assad was. Osama, Bashar, Saddam—they were all just bad men on the other side of the world to me. Now, I said to myself in disbelief, the US government is asking *us* to find a person who could personally exert influence on the president of Syria?

"Who do you suggest we use?" asked TAG. I could tell from his demeanor that his patience was close to an end.

"We can't help you with that. If we did, and if something went wrong, we can't have the US government held liable." Additionally, as they continued with their advice, they said, "We strongly recommend that you do not go public with Sam's case. Depending on who his captors are, if they feel public pressure to release Sam, they may just kill him instead."

In the awkward silence that followed, one of the officials spoke up. "You really need to manage your expectations," she said. "You may never see Sam alive again."

I responded, "Yes, I will, because I'm going to pray him home."

She replied, "Well, your prayer should be that Sam is dead, because if he is alive, he is being severely tortured."

With that, TAG and I exited the room, grabbed our phones out of the cubbies, and walked out of FBI headquarters in silence. When we got out onto the street, at the corner of Pennsylvania Avenue and Tenth Street, I turned to TAG and said, "We may never see Sam again, but this is *not* going to break up our marriage."

TAG nodded, still deep in thought.

The next thing I said to him was probably unfair, but I was feeling desperate. With both hands, I despairingly grabbed TAG by the collar.

"You bring our son home," I demanded.

TAG nodded again. "I will," he said.

SAM GOODWIN

When I first set foot in prison, my biggest fear was that I would be tortured, or worse. Now, after nine days of total seclusion, a new fear was paradoxically emerging—had I been utterly forgotten?

Being completely ignored in a foreign prison, unable to speak the local language and having zero meaningful contact with any other living soul, is a thoroughly excruciating experience. If I had at first felt like I had committed suicide and was yet somehow still alive, now I felt like a ghost haunting this unfamiliar place.

After nine or ten days, I began to wonder if anyone in the world knew where I was. Could the Syrian bureaucracy have somehow sucked me in and forgotten me? If I had a case file, had it been misplaced? The idea of slipping through the cracks and being stranded in this purgatory began to scare me. I craved attention. Or, if not attention, just for someone on earth to acknowledge that I still existed, that Sam Goodwin was still a person in the world.

This led me to a peculiar idea—I was going to pretend to be sick. It was a test, in a way, to see if anyone was actually thinking about me or if I had been entirely forgotten. It may have been a bad idea to draw attention to myself, but by this point I just had to know that someone knew I was still here, that even to my jailers I had some trace element of human value. Maybe I would even have the opportunity to get out of my cell for a while.

The next morning, when a minion came in to deliver food, I was lying on the floor on my stomach, faking that I was having trouble breathing. I had practiced my routine before the guard arrived and discovered that I could do it somewhat convincingly. As the guard set the food down, he couldn't help but notice me. But his reaction was minimal and he ducked out of the cell, leaving me alone as I pretended to be in the midst of a respiratory emergency.

Thirty seconds later, the same guard came back with two of his comrades in tow, all of them staring at me and speaking to one another in Arabic. To my relief, they helped me to my feet and we walked slowly to a small area down the corridor, where a table and chairs stood. They let me lie on the table until my breathing calmed down. Then, when I sat up, one of them patted me on the back, an oddly humanizing gesture in this totally dehumanized place. I wasn't sure what to do next, so I indicated that I was relatively okay again. This unfortunately put me on track to return to my cell. I may have only been out for about fifteen minutes in all, but it had at least been enough to show that my new world wasn't totally impervious to my existence.

A few days later, when I was again feeling forgotten, I staged another breathing episode. After being ignored for so long, I had developed a deep craving for even the smallest of attention. I knew these incidents were risky, though, as I would come to find out later.

This time, the guards brought me to a small rest area, a spot that seemed to be where they would go to take a break from serving meals, escorting inmates to the bathroom, and torturing people. I sat there wheezing for a while, gratified to see that two of the guards headed into my cell with a bucket and mops. It was at this point that the minions finally noticed that I had been peeing in the far corner of the L-shaped cell on the occasions when they failed to respond to my summons for the toilet. Nevertheless, I was happy to see the floor of my cell being cleaned. I must have become inured to the smell of ammonia and sweat, but the simple fact that someone cared enough about my well-being to mop it up buoyed my spirits a little.

A week and a half later, on day 23, I gave my fake asthma trick one more go. This time, frustrated and desperate, I was more dramatic and extreme with the performance. My entire thought process behind these episodes was that if I became sick enough in prison, perhaps then the Syrians would not want to deal with me anymore and would just send me home to the United States. In hindsight, this was probably naive, but with the information I had at the time and the horrendous situation I was in, I concluded it was worth a shot.

When the minions opened my door that morning, I was lying face down on the concrete floor, severely hyperventilating. Admittedly, I believe my acting was relatively impressive, and I had resolved to keep this up longer than before to see what would happen.

Two guards walked in to help me, and I acted as if I could hardly stand. They half carried, half led me to a different area of the dungeon, a second, larger common area where I could see guards and workers walking around with no shirts on, some mopping the floors and some just sort of hanging out. It was hard to observe anyone too closely as I was basically pretending to be dying, but it appeared to be a bizarre behind-the-scenes look at the inner workings of the facility.

They laid me on a table in the middle of the common area. I must have been there, wheezing, for about forty-five minutes when, out of nowhere, a guy I had never seen before approached me. He appeared to be slightly older than the usual minions, although he was wearing nothing to indicate that he was any sort of medical professional. This wasn't surprising. The only evidence I'd seen of a "doctor" in that place was a guy who would visit the cells once every few days with a suitcase full of pills. The medicine bottles had Arabic labels on them, which I obviously couldn't read. He would then offer them to me, as if I was going to take them without even knowing what they were. I later learned that they were sleeping pills, to allow the inmates to escape the horror of incarceration in the only way possible.

As I lay on the table panting, I noticed the newcomer holding an IV bag with a plastic tube. He reached up to clip it to the ceiling and then pulled out a large hypodermic needle. I was now in a jam. There was no way on earth I was going to let him put that needle inside me. Even if I somehow survived this ordeal, I had no desire to be infected for the rest of my life with HIV or some other disease found on contaminated needles in a Syrian dungeon. I immediately stopped panting and sat up. He looked straight at me. If he realized I had been faking it, it didn't register on his face. Maybe this happened all the time. Either way, he seemed indifferent about my miraculous recovery.

One of the younger guards led me back to my cell. In all, I had been out for nearly an hour. The experiment had been a moderate success. I learned that the minions, if pressed, would indeed take some sort of action to prevent me from dying, which certainly counted for something of note in this bleak underground prison.

All that being the case, I vowed to never fake being sick again.

DAVID GOODWIN, *27, Sam's youngest brother*

I think I was the first one in the family to say it out loud—maybe, just maybe, it would be better if Sam was dead.

If we knew what had happened to him and had a body to grieve over, that would probably make it easier for us to deal with everything.

In those first few weeks of despair and confusion, all of the alternatives seemed much, much worse. Not knowing if he was being tortured, if he was about to pop up on an ISIS or al-Qaeda beheading video, or if we might just never know what happened to him was daunting.

In addition to being deeply worried about Sam, I have to admit I was angry at him too. In my opinion, going to Syria was irresponsible, and I told him as much—*This is a bad idea.* I'm no expert on the Middle East. I play hockey for a living, but even to me, it seemed clear that going into a country at war with itself and riddled with jihadist terrorists was not a good thing to do.

As the days of uncertainty turned into weeks, I saw the pain my parents and our entire family were being forced to endure. That made me increasingly angry with my big brother for what I would characterize to be his poor decision-making. This isn't to say I wasn't sad or worried about him. I was, for sure, but he had made his own bed. I did everything I could to help the efforts to get him out. But as time passed, I realized that my primary focus was slowly shifting from finding Sam to taking care of my parents and making sure they survived the ordeal. My parents were seriously stressed. And for what? It wasn't as if Sam had been in Syria as an aid worker or a journalist, or even in the military. No, he'd gone as a traveler. Whenever people mentioned Austin Tice to us, I thought, "At least he was there trying to add something of value to the world." What was Sam there for? So yeah, I was pissed, on top of all the other turbulent emotions of the traumatic situation.

At certain points, I could voice these feelings to my mom, or to Steph or Betty, but most of the time I really had to rein in my emotions and stay supportive of my parents. The three remaining siblings and I decided early on that at least one of us should be at home with them at least once a week to help them get through this nightmare, even if it was just for a long weekend. Paul traveled from New York, Steph from Nashville, and I from State College, Pennsylvania, where I was spending the summer training for my upcoming hockey season.

In the summer of 2019, I was in the midst of a significant career move. I had spent the past two seasons playing professional hockey in Finland but had just signed with IK Oskarshamn, a team in the top Swedish Hockey League. This was a big deal. The SHL is considered to be among the top five pro hockey leagues in the world, so it was a major step up for me. I had arranged to spend the summer at my alma mater, Penn State, training and getting ready for the challenge. I was due to report to Sweden on July 31.

When Sam disappeared in May, it completely took over our lives. Everyone was forced to drop everything they were doing to help get him back. Betty almost canceled the trip of a lifetime to Portugal and Spain, and Steph wasn't sure if she should even get married that fall if Sam was still rotting in a jail cell in Syria. I was now having to fly back to St. Louis every couple of weeks, or get on endless conference calls with the FBI, or brainstorm with the WhatsApp group about ways to bring Sam home. In addition, given all the stress, I was having trouble sleeping at night, especially after a hard day of training. It was a huge emotional strain and the last thing a professional athlete wants when gearing up for a new season.

It wasn't that I didn't love Sam or didn't worry about him. He's my big brother and we've always been close. I'm three and a half years younger than Sam, with Paul in the middle. All three of us are close and were brought even closer by our shared love of hockey. We spent most of our childhood on the ice or on our driveway playing together. Sam and I talked on the phone a lot during the previous few years when I was in Finland and he was in Asia since we were only a couple of time zones apart, while the rest of our family was six or seven hours behind in the United States.

Few people could relate to me and what I was doing like Sam could. He'd had his own successful hockey career and knew the game inside and out. He was really excited that I was going to Sweden, but I still profoundly disagreed with what he had done.

Ultimately, after only a couple months in Sweden, my career there didn't work out, for a whole host of reasons, and I moved on to play in the UK, in Belfast. I can't lay that on Sam. It wasn't his fault, but it's certainly a data point.

LUKE HARTIG, *38, former US government official, hostage affairs expert*

TAG and Ann were clearly in shock that Sunday morning when I met them in the lobby of a DC hotel. That's very normal, of course. I've dealt with many people who have had to face the horror of having a loved one disappear in some foreign land, not knowing if they are dead or being tortured and abused. It's an extremely challenging thing to process emotionally. The families themselves are undergoing their own form of torture as a result of intense fear, doubt, and the possibility that they may never know what happened to their child, parent, or sibling.

Shock manifests itself in different ways. Ann was more withdrawn and not very communicative, which I later learned was far from usual. TAG was more talkative, keen to discuss the situation and find ways he might claw back some control. That's the thing about a kidnapping—while you might compare it to being diagnosed with a potentially fatal disease, in fact it is so far out of the normal range of experience for an average American that it is often hard to even begin to get your head around it. Yet this practice is becoming more and more common, especially with hostile and authoritarian states increasingly seeing Americans as valuable bargaining chips.

But there was another reason for the Goodwins' frustration. They had just had their first encounter with the US government, in particular the Hostage Recovery Fusion Cell. Interacting with the sprawling bureaucracies of our government can be a disorienting experience, even in the best of times. Not because our civil servants or law enforcement agents are ill-intentioned or incompetent, but because it is such a world unto itself, with its own particular ways of doing things. In Ann and TAG's case, it sounded like the experience had been particularly unpleasant. As a result, it quickly became clear that they wanted to see if I could bring any added value to their quest. If not, they wanted nothing more to do with me.

I'd worked for eight years on national security matters, including as a senior director for counterterrorism at the National Security Council in the Obama White House, and three years focusing heavily on hostage issues. In my final year there, we realized that US hostage policy was not working like it should and could, and needed a major overhaul. That was primarily because four young Americans had been murdered in Syria by ISIS—two journalists, James Foley and Steven Sotloff, and two humanitarian aid workers, Kayla Mueller and Peter Kassig.

There had been several unsuccessful military missions to try to rescue them, carried out by highly skilled special operations forces. None had worked. In July 2014, a raid was carried out by our commandos on an Islamic State hideout at an oil facility near Raqqa, in northern Syria. Its mission was to free James Foley and other hostages thought to be there, but the captives had been moved just days earlier.

A month later, ISIS released a brutal video showing them beheading James Foley, the forty-year-old freelance journalist. A month later, they did the same with his colleague Steven Sotloff. In November, they proceeded to murder Peter Kassig, who had been kidnapped a year earlier while delivering food and medical supplies to refugees in eastern Syria. ISIS was clearly spacing out the killings to maximize international media attention. That was designed to both intimidate any foes and also help recruit new fighters from around the world.

In February 2015, ISIS announced that Kayla Mueller had been killed during a Jordanian airstrike on a building where the terror network had been holding her. It was hard to know exactly what had killed her. It could have been the bomb or it could have been ISIS, but regardless, it was determined that she was dead.

The unsuccessful attempts to free US hostages included other cases too, notably a special operations forces raid in Yemen to try to rescue US journalist Luke Somers and a South African teacher and relief worker named Pierre Korkie. They were being held by al-Qaeda in the Arabian Peninsula, a particularly dangerous offshoot of the terrorist organization. The US military launched a raid to free Somers, but during the operation, in December 2014, the militants killed both hostages.

In addition to that, a US operation targeting an al-Qaeda compound near the Afghanistan-Pakistan border accidentally killed an American hostage, aid worker Warren Weinstein, in January 2015. The seventy-three-year-old was four days away from completing a seven-year-stint with the US Agency for International Development when he was abducted in 2011. The strike also killed an Italian humanitarian worker, Giovanni Lo Porto.

Clearly, the United States' hostage policy needed a serious rethink. I was part of the team that spent months working on the review, which President Barack Obama signed off on in June 2015.

One of the central changes we made was establishing the Hostage Recovery Fusion Cell, to get away from the disjointed intel sharing and operational coordination that is so common among government agencies and to allow experts to come together, in the same space, to share what they know and discuss approaches. Another focus was to try to move away from the bias toward risky military operations and to see if there might be other ways to secure the release of captives, perhaps through diplomatic channels or third-party negotiators, such as local organizations or community leaders, or by running clandestine intelligence operations. We also created a new deliberative body at the White House called the Hostage Response Group, to keep up with the HRFC's work.

One of the changes was in how we dealt with the families of the hostages. Until then, they had been largely an addendum, at best a source of primary information about the missing person, and then more or less overlooked. In this new approach, we would work directly with them and bring them into the process. That presented some challenges, of course. Investigators in government agencies aren't always best equipped to deal with grief-stricken relatives or, as we were to discover in TAG and Ann's case, singularly determined ones.

In our review, we had also introduced a family coordinator to help deal with relatives more effectively. This proved to be a mixed blessing. On one hand, it meant families were kept more in the loop. On the other, many relatives are often simply confused when they are offered counseling or relationship support by the government. They will quite often say, "We already have a pastor," or "We have a therapist." What they expect from the government is to get their loved one back as quickly as possible, which is rarely a simple process.

When an authoritarian government with which we have friendly relations, such as Egypt or Saudi Arabia, arrests a US citizen, it is a relatively straightforward process to get people released. But when someone disappears in a hostile country, like Russia, China, North Korea, Iran, or Syria, it is a very different matter.

The first problem in Sam's case was that initially, no one seemed to have any idea if he had been taken by the Syrian regime or some nonstate actor, such as a terrorist group or other militant force. By 2019, Syria was a patchwork of competing forces and ethnicities, which complicated our information-gathering process. Personally, I was surprised that he had been taken in a predominantly Kurdish-controlled area, although I knew there were pockets of territory in the northeast held by the Assad regime.

From some of my previous work, I had a good understanding of Syria's prison system. It seemed likely to me that if the regime had taken Sam, he would be held in the military intelligence prison system. That was good on one hand, because Sam was less likely to be seriously abused or executed there than if he was being held in one of the more notorious regime jails like Sednaya, a facility just outside Damascus where torture and murder were rampant. According to the Syrian Observatory for Human Rights, a staggering thirty thousand detainees have been killed there, or died of a mixture of abuse and neglect. The downside of the military prison system is that they are black holes, with almost no information ever leaking out. These are places where you could vanish off the radar, potentially for a very long time, and there'd be no way to even verify if Sam was alive or actually being held by the regime.

I told TAG and Ann that I would help them try to establish where Sam might be and would use my own contacts in the world of government and hostages to ensure this was a top priority. In addition, I advised them that one of the most important things they needed to do, which was well within their capabilities, was to increase pressure on the US government to act. They needed to contact their senators and any other key figures in Congress who might be able to help gain resources for their cause. However, they had been advised against doing this by someone in the Fusion Cell, who warned them that an absolute blackout was needed. I told them that the senators and their staff would be more than happy to meet them and would be able to deal with the issue in absolute confidentiality.

We also discussed the advantages and risks of a press campaign, leaning heavily on the insight of my colleague Emily Lenzner, a renowned communications and public affairs specialist in Washington. On one hand, this would raise awareness of Sam's case and increase pressure on our government to act. The downside, however, was that it might make Sam appear more valuable to whoever was holding him and potentially prompt them to move him somewhere even more hidden away.

TAG, Ann, and I talked for an hour before they had to catch a flight back to St. Louis. One last thing I promised them was a meeting with my new boss, David Bradley, who at the time was the chairman of Atlantic Media and owner of the National Journal Group, where I worked. During the turbulent period of the Arab Spring, when nations across the Middle East were rising up against their autocratic rulers in 2011 and 2012, David had been very active in trying to get abducted journalists freed, since journalists are generally in the highest-risk group for kidnapping. In 2011, he worked to secure the release of freelance reporter Clare Gillis, who was being held in Libya by forces loyal to Muammar Gaddafi. That process also led to the liberation of James Foley and several other reporters being held by the crumbling regime. A year later, David had worked hard when Foley was again captured, this time in Syria, along with several other Western reporters and humanitarian workers. This time, unfortunately, he was not as successful.

David's work had brought him into contact with me, and I was so impressed with his approach that I went over to the *National Journal* to work for him. As my meeting with TAG and Ann wound up, I told them that the next time they were in town, I would introduce them to David. They thought about it, then agreed. Apparently they trusted me enough to keep me in the loop, and trust is key in this business.

ANN GOODWIN

TAG was pretty sure the Fusion Cell would be a bust, so he had wisely set up a number of other meetings over the course of our long weekend in DC. He again asked Ben Stephan to join and help us maneuver the city. Ben had spent much of his life around large bureaucratic institutions, since the majority of his mother's professional career was working for the World Bank. Also, since the nuncio to the United States, whom we were due to meet, is from France, we figured it was a good idea to have Ben with us, since he is a native French speaker.

Our first stop was at the offices of the International Committee of the Red Cross. Of course, the ICRC is among the most influential humanitarian groups in the world and not only delivers aid to people in crisis situations but also, crucially for us, often has access to prisons in authoritarian states. The woman we met with was a "global protection officer" who told us that the group had limited access to just a few prisons in Syria. She pulled out a three-by-five notecard and asked me to write Sam a message, on the off chance that one of their people might come across him during a prison visit. I was stunned. What do I write to my missing son, who may be in fear for his life? The officer warned me not to write anything that might be misconstrued as a coded message, so I just kept it simple and heartfelt. "Dear Sam, We love you very much. God is caring for you. Mom and Dad."

I felt quite overwhelmed even writing those few words. I vowed, right there and then, that if my son didn't show up soon I would join the International Committee of the Red Cross. As a registered nurse, I would try to get into Syrian prisons myself to find Sam. I later learned that Austin Tice's mother, Debra, had lived in Syria for three months after her son was taken by the regime, trying to find him. Alas, to no avail.

We also met with a kind woman named Liz Frank, the executive director of an organization called Hostage US, which supports families of American citizens who have been wrongfully detained or taken hostage abroad. I hadn't realized until then that every year, around two hundred Americans are taken hostage. These could be journalists, aid workers, travelers, or people on business. For example, years ago in Colombia, there were so many people being kidnapped that there was actually a radio station set up for them so that loved ones could send messages to abducted family members, who might be missing for years. The radio station ran for twenty-five years and only shut down in 2018, after the government signed a peace deal with the rebel guerrillas.

I learned that Americans today are being wrongfully detained in a handful of places around the world. China, for example, holds several Americans on allegations of spying, as do Iran and Venezuela. The Syrian government is also believed to be holding at least one other American: journalist Austin Tice. Majd Kamalmaz, a psychotherapist from Virginia who was treating traumatized war refugees when he was arrested at a government checkpoint in 2017, was reported dead in 2024. "Tragically, he did not survive the brutal conditions of the prisons," the Bring Our Families Home Campaign said. Hostage-taking has become a serious weapon in the armory of authoritarian regimes trying to push back against US sanctions or embargoes. Now it appeared my son had become one of them.

Hostage US is unique in that it provides all kinds of emotional and practical support for the families of people who have been kidnapped. Since being taken hostage is such an unusual and disturbing experience, it often helps to speak to the few people who understand the strain it puts on a family. The organization also provides counseling for hostages when they are released, helping them readjust after isolation, torture, and often severe malnutrition. It was a sobering snapshot of the long struggle looming ahead for my family, and that was if we managed to get Sam back.

Unfortunately, on that trip, we missed the Vatican envoy. DC's infamous traffic snarl-ups meant that we were late getting to the embassy, and the nuncio had only a fifteen-minute opening. But we left a letter with him to be forwarded to the Holy Father, begging him to intercede on our behalf.

When we flew back to St. Louis at the end of that June weekend, we could at least reassure ourselves we were leaving no stone unturned.

SAM GOODWIN

When I arrived in Syria in May 2019, I spoke virtually zero Arabic, with the exception of basic phrases like *shukran* ("thank you") and *salam alaykum* ("peace be upon you"—a common greeting in the Arab world). While in solitary confinement, I had limited human interaction. But the brief encounters I did have led to me learning a few Arabic words, two of which became particularly discouraging. The first was *mofi*, which I came to understand can be translated to "don't have." Whenever I asked for something from the guards, like a toothbrush or a pen and paper or more food, they would respond with "Mofi." Through context clues from many of these incidents, I began to figure out its meaning.

Mofi, however, pales in comparison to the word that became the most infuriating to hear while in solitary confinement. Throughout my time in Branch 215, I desperately asked the guards many questions, like if I could make a phone call or if I could speak to someone in English or if I could leave Syria and go home. In response, they would often just smile and say, "*Bukra*." I heard this word a million times before I had any idea what it meant, but as time passed and I continued to gather information, I learned that *bukra* is the Arabic word for "tomorrow." The moment I figured this out, I thought of the small signs that restaurants and bars in the Western world sometimes humorously hang in their windows that read Free Beer Tomorrow. Responding to my requests with *bukra* was a cruel captivity tactic, and one I will always associate with the guards at Branch 215.

On day 14 of my incarceration in the Damascus dungeon, the guards came to move me. That was when I truly discovered the nature of where I was being held. A guard came into my cell and indicated with hand gestures that I had to grab all my things. Since I didn't even have so much as a toothbrush, that didn't take long. I just picked up my two blankets and followed him, full of trepidation. Was I leaving jail? Or was he leading me to some lower circle of hell?

We didn't go far, just down the hallway to another cell, around a dogleg maybe fifty yards from the first. I was escorted into a new cell, this one even smaller than where I had come from. But it did have a few advantages. The first was that it had its own toilet, a simple hole in the corner of the concrete floor. That meant I no longer had to summon the guards to go to the bathroom, even if those episodes had been somewhat of a relief, just to get out of the cell.

Even better than the toilet, however, was that this cell had a tiny sliver of a window to the outside world. It wasn't much, a crack of dusty glass above my reach, half-obscured by a pipe and cobwebs, but it allowed me to see if it was day or night, and that was a significant psychological improvement. I could finally accurately track the passage of time. One of the first things I did here was find a small rock and use it to carve a new calendar into the cell wall.

I quickly discovered that there was a huge downside to my new home, in addition to the distant scent of sewage coming from the toilet. I was now closer to the center of the prison, and I could hear just about everything that was happening in the facility. The screams, the crying, right down to the sound of blows landing on my terrified fellow prisoners in the adjacent cells. It even sounded like some of the prisoners were women and children. If my previous cell was in Coney Island, I had now been moved to Times Square.

The next morning, I heard the start of terrifying brutality being systematically carried out in this central part of the dungeon. It began with the distant sound of a metal bolt being pulled back on a cell door at the far end of the corridor. A second later, there would be a frantic bout of screaming for about thirty seconds, then silence.

Quickly following this was the sound of a second deadbolt being drawn back and more awful shouts and yells. This went on, cell by cell, as the guards worked their way down the hall toward me, opening each door, beating the hell out of each inmate and then slamming the door as they left. I don't think I knew what fear was until I heard a grown man screaming for his life. The sound hollowed me out. As they got closer and closer to my cell, I could even hear the creak of the hinges and the thud of batons on flesh. It was beyond terrifying, in part because I couldn't actually see anything.

In my whole time in Branch 215, I never saw another inmate, only heard their screams of pain and terror. The Syrian officials knew I could hear everything from my cell. I sat on the floor, back to the wall, too frightened to move. Next door, I could hear the cell door open. The screaming, so close to me now, was unbearable. I was frozen in place, as far away from the door as possible, my knees pulled up to my chest and my arms around my knees. My mind was a blank slate of anticipation.

Then I heard the bolt on my cell slide back, and the door slowly opened. A large man stood in the doorway, a man I'd never seen before. Unlike the minions who brought me food every day, this man was older and wearing a green military-style uniform and a forage cap on his head. He looked a bit like Qassim Soleimani, the commander of the Islamic Revolutionary Guard Corps in Iran who would be killed in a US airstrike in Iraq the following year.

A few of the minions stood behind him, their faces as expressionless as his. There was no club in his hand, so maybe one of them was holding it. I was transfixed by the man, who stepped into my cell and stood there for a long moment, staring at me as I huddled on the floor. Then he gave me a half wave from his temple, almost like a casual salute, and said, "Samwell."

I think I may have managed to croak out a feeble "yes" before he turned on his heel and left. The door slammed and I heard the deadbolt slide back into place. A second later, the door of my other neighbor creaked open and the poor inmate next door started screaming for his life.

I sat there, utterly emptied by fear, for a long time, as the sound of the beatings and creaking doors receded down the hallway and finally ended.

That routine would be repeated at the same time, every day, for as long as I was in the dungeon. Of course, I couldn't help but wonder, when was my turn?

LUKE HARTIG

Most people are familiar with the notion of "six degrees of separation," the idea that in our increasingly interconnected world, you could find a link to just about anyone on the planet through friends of friends, or at least casual acquaintances that connect us all. The concept has been around for decades and can sometimes be a fun game to play at dinner parties.

Obviously, the global population has drastically increased in recent decades and it's impossible to definitively say if everyone is separated from, say, a Mongolian yak herder by just five people, but it certainly provides an illustration of one thing—you don't yet know whom you might know.

This was one of the reasons I went to work for David Bradley at the *National Journal* after my stint in government, because in addition to having worked for years on hostage recovery, I also had strong knowledge of how social networks actually function, as this is a core component of counterterrorism analysis. These days, I run a business for David that, among other things, helps our clients map the social networks essential to their business objectives. We understand public policy and how people are connected. We use that mapping and knowledge to help advocates with their engagement strategies, from using data to uncover emerging power centers to targeting influential figures in fields such as health care, finance, and beyond.

David is always willing to help out in hostage situations. It has become one of his many centers of expertise, and something of a crusade. Before we met TAG and Ann, he and I sat down and tried to whiteboard out how we could get them close to key Syrian power brokers, potentially even Assad himself. As strange as it may seem now, with cities devastated by his armies and helicopters raining down barrel bombs—even chemical weapons being used against civilians—Assad was once seen as a great hope for the Middle East.

This was in part because he was never actually meant to be president. His father, Hafez—the man whose statue had borne silent witness to Sam's abduction on the streets of Qamishli—had long groomed his elder son, Bassel, to take over that role. Bassel was cast in the same strongman role as his father, while Bashar left Syria to become an ophthalmologist in London. There, he married a beautiful British woman of Syrian origin and settled down to practice as an eye doctor far from the power struggles of the Middle East. By all accounts, he was a good doctor and always played down his close links to the regime. Had his brother not died in a car accident, he probably would have stayed there. As it was, Bashar was recalled to Syria to undergo a crash course on running the family dictatorship, starting with a stint as commander of Syrian forces in Lebanon, which had effectively occupied its tiny neighbor since the days of Lebanon's bloody civil war.

In 2000, when Hafez died of a heart attack, Bashar succeeded him as president, raising hopes that a westernized doctor might have a slightly more liberal view of ruling the country. Those hopes seemed to be borne out in the early days of his presidency, when he withdrew Syrian forces from Lebanon in 2005 following a peaceful uprising by the Lebanese people, known as the Cedar Revolution, in response to the assassination of popular former prime minister Rafic Hariri. Hariri's car was blown up outside the plush St. George Hotel in the heart of Beirut. Two members of the Iranian-backed group Hezbollah were later convicted of the killing by a UN court, although some hinted at links to Assad, whose country is also closely allied with Tehran.

As time passed, the regime didn't soften its line. Instead, Assad himself seemed to harden his tone, as he was surrounded by his father's hard-line aides and advisers, who inducted him into the grim realities of running a police state. Then in 2011, the Arab Spring swept through the region. It began when a poor Tunisian man selling fruit by the roadside had his wares confiscated by the police in December 2010. The twenty-six-year-old had been peddling his goods out of desperation, unable to find a job amid a stagnating economy in a country beset by corruption and ruled by President Zine el-Abidine Ben Ali, who had come to power in a bloodless coup almost a quarter of a century earlier. An hour after losing his only possessions, Mohamed Bouazizi doused himself in gasoline and set himself on fire. His death triggered a massive upswell of anger across the country, with huge demonstrations in the streets demanding change. When Ben Ali fled the country, a spark was set across a region long ruled by aging strongmen who had for decades jailed, beaten, or even murdered any opposition. Protests erupted in Egypt, Libya, Jordan, and the Gulf States, and across North Africa. It was the most tumultuous upheaval in the region since decolonization in the middle of the twentieth century.

It took some time for that spark to catch fire in Syria, mainly because Syria was one of the most repressive and efficient police states of the Arab world. In 1982, when the opposition group known as the Muslim Brotherhood staged an uprising in Hama, Hafez al-Assad showed no mercy. He sent his troops to besiege the city, killing as many as forty thousand people in the monthlong battle. Now the Syrian people were understandably more wary of taking to the streets against such a power.

Nevertheless, the spark came when a group of schoolboys were arrested for spraying anti-Assad graffiti on a wall in the southern town of Daraa, close to the Jordanian border. They were reportedly beaten and had their fingernails ripped out. In response, protesters took to the streets and security forces opened fire on them. Far from being cowed, the protesters grew in number and the demonstrations spread across the country. Soon, Syria was engulfed in a complex revolution that would see the regime fighting a pro-democracy opposition, Islamist extremists declaring their own caliphate, and Kurds taking control of territory where their people lived. Eventually, US special forces, which were already based in Syria to support the counter-ISIS effort, would become increasingly engaged while Russian troops and warplanes would enter the fray to prop up Assad, bombing hospitals and causing a vast exodus of people into neighboring Turkey and on into Europe.

Navigating a way through this complex web to get close enough to Assad to exert some influence in favor of Sam would not be easy. David and I drew up several diagrams mapping out the people we knew who would know people closer to the heart of Assad's power base.

In one of them, we laid out Assad's inner circle—the president himself, his younger brother Maher, and his closest security aide, Ali Mamlouk. Any one of them, we thought, could release Sam with a mere phone call. In the next circle was Asma, Bashar's British-born wife. She was promising because she still had ties to the United Kingdom. Next to her was Assad's trusted media adviser, Bouthaina Shaaban. She had a daughter who was living in Florida and also was in contact with a number of Arab American officials, including a former US ambassador to Syria and the head of the Arab American Institute in DC.

Also in that second circle were powerful business leaders and media owners—a bit like the Syrian equivalent of David himself—who had contacts to lower-level officials who in turn were known to Western journalists that we knew who worked in the Middle East. There was also the grand mufti of Damascus, the highest Sunni religious authority in the country, who we knew had recent contact with a Spanish diplomat. Once mapped out, the impenetrable regime in Damascus suddenly seemed a lot more accessible. Certainly, far fewer than six degrees of separation.

PART V

RUSSIAN ROULETTE

TAG GOODWIN

My plan from the beginning was to cover all bases and follow every possible lead, no matter how tenuous it seemed. This approach, of course, occasionally led me into some seemingly treacherous waters.

A few weeks after Sam's disappearance, one of his closest childhood friends, David Makowski, got in touch with our son Paul. It was Paul's main job to field all the inquiries from Sam's many friends around the world, lots of whom were starting to ask why Sam was all of a sudden silent on social media and not answering phone calls. Paul was being forced to make up so many stories about Sam that he was having trouble keeping them all straight in his head. Even though by this point, Paul had become a pro at making up these mythical tales, the excuses about Sam traveling in areas with unreliable internet or phone networks were beginning to wear thin. Paul, sick of the whole business, blurted out the truth to David. That was when David called me and suggested he might be able to help.

David, a former pro hockey player himself, informed me that his wife, Carrie, has a friend who is closely affiliated with a group of veteran Navy SEALs. They founded a company that acts as trusted security advisers for Texas oilmen heading to the less secure parts of the Middle East. Carrie said that, as well as escorting oil execs, he and some of his former special forces buddies occasionally did special missions, such as hostage rescue or close protection services, as private contractors. This made me wonder—did I want to talk to them?

It sounded like a long shot, since the US government itself didn't seem to have the slightest clue as to where Sam was. But I gave it a go anyway and spoke to Carrie's friend. Interestingly, and without providing many details, the guy said he and his group somehow had access to the daily classified briefings that were shown every day to President Trump and that Sam's situation was being mentioned in some of these meetings. I was skeptical about this reported access but continued to hear him out.

As the conversation progressed, he asked if I could pay $1 million for a mission to get into Syria and spring Sam out of jail—a $500,000 down payment now, and then the balance paid upon completion of the mission. He sounded confident in his ability to be successful.

It's very hard for someone like me, a businessman in St. Louis, to gauge whether a group of freelancing former Navy SEALs might be able to do such a thing. You hear of the incredible ops they carry out, rescue missions or coups and even assassinations, but it's not like they hand out a résumé with a list of all these borderline-legal activities. There are no Yelp reviews. In addition, the Fusion Cell had warned us that as soon as word of Sam's situation got out, there'd be any number of people trying to chisel money out of us. In the end, I decided to put the DIY rescue mission on a back burner for now and return to the SEALs if our other channels ran into the ground. But I didn't say no to them.

One of Sam's other closest friends, Nick Gastorf, got married in Dallas while Sam was missing. Months earlier, Sam had RSVP'd yes to attending. Nick is one of Sam's best friends from high school. When he and Nick were sophomores in 2004, Nick's father tragically passed away from a heart attack. During the funeral, Nick asked Sam to stand beside him on the altar as he delivered the eulogy. The two of them had remained in touch over the years, even when Sam worked in Asia for the better part of a decade. Needless to say, this was not a wedding that Sam would have missed. So when Sam didn't show up in Dallas, and more significantly, didn't even reach out to Nick to say he wouldn't be there, Nick got in touch with Paul to find out what was going on. This was another example of one of the many unforeseen communication challenges that Paul and the rest of our family were being forced to manage, few of which I believe would intuitively be linked with a kidnapping but all of which were our reality.

In addition to the SEALs, another seemingly shady line of inquiry led us to the office of the Russian ambassador to Syria. I had been brainstorming with Rob, who had flown down from Toronto for a weekend of tactical planning, and told him that we potentially needed to find a Russian hook, since Moscow was actively propping up the Assad regime, either shielding it diplomatically at the UN or sending in troops, mercenaries, or fighter-bombers to do its dirty work. This was when Rob remembered that Sam knew a Russian businessman whom he had met while playing hockey in Dubai. They had connected through a mutual friend named Aaron, who was living in the United Kingdom and who was trying, with this Russian man Victor, to establish a Russian-dominated Kontinental Hockey League team in the United Arab Emirates. The KHL is considered to be second only to the NHL, so we figured Victor might have some useful connections in Moscow.

Throughout the course of our team's efforts, as we strategized together and spoke with people from across the US government and beyond, we would often be asked if anyone on our team had a contact in a particular country or city, or with a particular group of people who might be able to help. In response to these inquiries, we frequently found ourselves looking around at one another and concluding, "We don't, but Sam probably would." Professionally, up to this point, Sam had worked in business development and investor relations. He made a living connecting dots and building relationships. Pair this with a likable personality and extensive world travels—Sam had friends in what seemed to quite literally be everywhere. This connection to Victor through the Dubai hockey network was one of several examples. Ironically and frustratingly, the person who we believed could be the most helpful to our worldwide search and rescue operation was the same person we were searching for and trying to rescue.

Nevertheless, Rob called Aaron, who promised to talk to Victor. As it happened, Victor said he actually knew the current Russian ambassador to Syria, since this man had been posted in the UAE before Damascus, which is where Victor got to know him. He promised to reach out, which felt like a huge breakthrough. When Ann informed the Fusion Cell of this, they were flabbergasted. "How did you get connected with the Russian ambassador to Syria?" one of them asked. "We can't even do that!" We quickly heard from Victor that the ambassador had agreed to make inquiries.

Unfortunately, nothing is ever quite as it seems in these circles. Aaron started receiving oddly contradictory, vaguely worded text messages from Victor, which he said had come from the ambassador. The first one was very straightforward. "Sam is not in Damascus—100 percent," which flew in the face of everything we had heard from US experts, like Luke Hartig and the FBI. Then another one was downright gnostic: "Sam is where he roams." Now what the hell did *that* mean?

Even though Victor was acting as Sam's friend and former hockey teammate, the Russian ambassador would certainly have his own agenda set by Moscow, which was most likely not favorable to any US interests. I asked my friend and colleague Gregg, who was based in Abu Dhabi, to go and meet Victor to see what he thought. Gregg reported that he struggled to get a clear read on Victor and his efforts.

It was important to keep in mind that the Syrian government is a complex web of competing factions in itself, as Luke reminded us. It was reasonable to believe that the person in the government whom the Russian ambassador approached had no idea his own government was even holding Sam. Generally speaking, it was all convoluted chaos, and we did our best to continue pushing forward.

Needless to say, by this point, the rescue operation had become an official, round-the-clock mission. Sam's Instagram handle was @Searching4Sam, a name that was appropriate, given all the travel content he posted. Now, of course, for us, this had taken on a whole new meaning. Our WhatsApp group consisted of core task force members Rob Martini, Luke Hartig, Ben Stephan, Father Vigoa, Emily Lenzner (a strategic communications executive and colleague of Luke's), Tim McAtee (a Texas-based security professional working as the director of global security for International Medical Corps), David, Paul, Ann, and myself. We spoke daily, usually multiple times. After these discussions, Tim and I would often have our own follow-up call. He, like everyone in the group, was a steadfast and remarkably dependable confidant for me during the toughest of times. For expediency and confidentiality, Rob suggested we give ourselves the code name "Team SG23," SG for Sam Goodwin and the 23 representing Sam's college hockey jersey number. The Team SG23 members put their lives on hold to support me twenty-four seven. It was an outstanding unit.

So outstanding, in fact, that an unforeseen consequence came as a result of the efforts of our group. We didn't know it at the time, but at some point in late June, the US government internally decided to intentionally scale back their engagement on Sam's case as a result of, and to not interfere with, what they considered to be unprecedented headway being made by the Goodwin family. National Security Council official and experienced hostage negotiator Dustin Stewart later said that the Goodwins' efforts were unlike anything he typically experiences. To this day, part of me wonders if the government just says this now because they realize they were severely outpaced in a geopolitical chess game by ordinary citizens from the Midwest, or if they actually made this strategic determination. We don't know.

In any case, to be fair, it wasn't as if they did nothing. Robert

O'Brien, the special presidential envoy for hostage affairs, known by its acronym, SPEHA, sent his deputy, Julia Nesheiwat, to Rome to meet with the Vatican about efforts to get Sam out. She then flew to Prague to speak to the Czech ambassador to Syria, Eva Filipi, whose embassy was handling US interests in Syria in the absence of our diplomatic ties. O'Brien agreed to meet us in his own office in DC when we were next in the capital. He gave us his personal phone number and told us to call whenever we needed anything, which was very considerate. While meeting with Robert, we gave him a small scrapbook of Sam's travel photos from around the world. Ann had compiled these images as part of our persistent effort to humanize Sam and do all we could to ensure that the narrative among the government and others we met aligned with the true nature of his travels, something we learned is often crucial in hostage cases.

We then saw on Robert's desk that he had a deck of cards, like baseball cards. When we asked what they were, he said they were all US citizens being held hostage or "wrongfully detained," which is just a diplomatic euphemism for being held hostage by a contentious foreign government.

"That looks like a lot of people," Ann said, eyeing the deck. There must have been at least twenty cards there.

He grimaced. "Yeah. There are lots of Americans being wrongfully detained."

On the heels of our meeting with O'Brien, Ben managed to arrange a video call for us with the former US ambassador to Syria, Robert Ford. He hadn't spent too much time in Syria, since he had been appointed right before the Arab Spring in 2011. The regime subsequently accused him of supporting and inciting the rebels, prompting fears in Washington that Assad might try to assassinate him. He withdrew from Syria shortly after that and left the diplomatic service a few years later. When we spoke to him, he came across as one of the most pessimistic of all the people we had met so far, which, given his experience with Syria, was deeply disturbing.

"Why would you reach out to me?" he asked us. "Assad hates me."

His prognosis was equally gloomy. "You will not get Sam out," he told us. "The only person who might be able to get him out is me and I can't do it."

That was certainly not what we wanted to hear. We thanked him politely and never spoke to him again.

STEPHANIE (STEPH) GOODWIN

One of the most challenging things about this whole situation was not being able to tell anyone what was going on. Imagine there is something awful weighing on you every day and grinding your family down, but you can't speak about it. The FBI had been very insistent about the fact that elevating Sam's public profile and the news of his disappearance could lead to him being killed by the regime or add to his value as a hostage. If he had been kidnapped by some criminal gang, they might just try to sell him to al-Qaeda or ISIS, which had been known to pay millions of dollars for hostages. It was a whole industry out there, we were told, and when these gangs got their hands on someone, it was almost always for one purpose—a videotaped beheading.

We had to be extremely diligent with our communication, keeping it strictly among our immediate family, Team SG23, and the growing number of people helping us in our effort. Every day, sometimes multiple times a day, Dad would host a conference call with Team SG23, giving updates, looking for feedback, and attempting to identify new contacts to expand the network. My siblings and I sometimes joined in, but we couldn't tell any friends or extended family members about our nightmare.

We have a large and very sociable extended family. Dad has ten siblings. Our cousins, uncles, aunts, and grandparents were having summer birthday parties, weddings, and family reunions as our world was simultaneously falling apart. I was scheduled to get married later that year, in November, to my fiancé, Matt. Could I even go ahead with it if Sam wasn't there? Sam had already missed our engagement party on June 1, and it took every ounce of my energy that evening to be present with our friends and family when all I could think about was Sam. Missing him again at our wedding would cast a huge shadow over what was supposed to be an even more joyful occasion. On the other hand, could I realistically postpone everything and tell the guests that they had to cancel the flights they had already booked? On top of this, could I do all of that without telling them *why*? These aren't things that might normally be associated with a kidnapping, but they were all very real for our family and me.

My brother David was upset with Sam. He'd never been a big supporter of Sam's travel journeys and would often grumble about why couldn't he just get on a normal career path like everyone else. That said, David—who is a professional hockey player in Europe—has exactly the job Sam always wanted but was denied due to his serious concussion injuries. David was worried about the toll this whole thing was taking on our parents, saying that the trauma and the massive workload on Dad's shoulders could take years off his life.

At one point, maybe a week into the ordeal, David said it might be better if we already knew that Sam was dead. That way we could have closure and grieve. The agony of having no idea if our brother was being held in a cage somewhere by al-Qaeda—or might one day turn up in an orange jumpsuit to be beheaded on camera, or might just disappear forever into the Syrian prison system, accused of spying, and no one would know anything until the regime fell fifty years from now—became too much to bear, and we worried how it would affect our parents.

David's anger may just have been his way of coping. When he was very little, he always looked up to his big brother and would follow him around and try to do whatever Sam did, like becoming an expert hockey player. It was clear that he was really hurting and desperately wanted his big brother to come home.

The same weekend in June that my parents had their first meeting in DC with the Fusion Cell, our family was scheduled to all be together at our cousin's wedding in Indianapolis. Obviously, Dad and Mom didn't make it, so I went with my siblings Paul and Betty instead. When we showed up to the ceremony, our extended family members from my dad's side were asking me, "Where's TAG? Why did he back out at the last minute?" We told them that he had a huge work project and had to stay home to deal with it. "What about Ann?"

they asked. We told them Mom was also tied up, with end-of-year school business. I don't know how convincing we were, but they had no choice but to buy it. Betty jokingly downplayed their absence. "Oh, who cares about Dad anyway?" she said. "Even if he were here he'd be in bed by eight o'clock!"

Later, Rob Goodwin, our dad's brother, cornered Betty during the reception and said in a conspiratorial whisper, "I know TAG and Ann are in DC for Sam's CIA graduation. You can let me in on the secret now, Betty. We all know he's in the CIA. This whole travel thing is fake." Betty tried to laugh off and deny his comments since we all know they're not true, but deep down she worried that if one of Sam's own relatives held this belief, might the Syrians also draw the same conclusion?

My fiancé, Matt, who works as VP of sales for an organic foods business, was a huge support through all of this. As is the case with most average Americans, there had never been much reason for us to understand the details of hostages who'd been murdered by ISIS or the hundreds of thousands of Syrians who'd been killed in the civil war. I was not able to digest it all, but Matt is unflappable. I relied on him to read about everything online and only share the information that might not plunge me into despair. Matt, thoughtful as always, tried to focus on the positive—or at least less negative—stories. He shared that there had recently been some German guy who'd been held by the Syrian regime and was released. The conditions had been tough, but he made it.

Not once did he mention the names Austin Tice or James Foley. It wasn't much protection against the horrors we feared were coming down the pike, but it got me through those anxious first weeks of the ordeal.

LUKE HARTIG

In 2023, four years after Sam's case, three British men were being held in Afghanistan by the Taliban, which once again had taken control of the country after the US withdrawal two years earlier.

Only two of them were publicly named. One was identified as charity medic Kevin Cornwell. The fifty-three-year-old was working in the country for a nongovernmental organization that provides health care for Afghan citizens.

The other was identified as twenty-three-year-old Miles Routledge, a self-described "danger tourist" who had built up a sizeable social media following by traveling to dangerous places like Ukraine after the Russian invasion, South Sudan, and Snake Island off the coast of Brazil, which is home to as many as four thousand golden lancehead vipers, one of the world's deadliest species of snake and whose venom can kill a person in under an hour. Routledge had actually been evacuated by British forces during the final NATO withdrawal in the summer of 2021, when the Taliban had taken control. Instead of chalking that one up as a lucky escape, he later went back and was captured.

Now, ask yourself this: If you saw this report, where would your sympathies lie? For the vast majority of people, they would feel sympathy for Cornwell, the aid worker, and roll their eyes at Routledge.

But now consider this: In early 2002, just a few months after the Taliban had been toppled by the US military in the wake of the 9/11 attacks, a twenty-nine-year-old British man named Rory Stewart walked alone across the lawless and unstable country for thirty-six days, with zero protection besides passable knowledge of Dari and relying on the hospitality of local Afghans in the villages he passed through. Stewart, a British diplomat on leave from the Foreign Office, had decided to walk across Asia on his sabbatical, and the turmoil in Afghanistan wasn't going to stop him. He later wrote a bestselling book about his experience, called *The Places in Between*, and went on to become a professor at Harvard and a member of the British Parliament, and later served in several ministerial posts in the British government.

Now ask yourself this: Where does his experience fit into the public consciousness? It is a question worth asking, because narrative is key when dealing with hostages. The line between a romantic "adventurer" and a "danger tourist" is one that can easily become blurred in the public eye. Part of our job with Sam was to shape that narrative, and TAG and Ann were tireless advocates on this front. The scrapbook of Sam's travel photos that they handed out in many of their DC meetings was a fundamental and effective example of this. While some people who didn't know him might have rolled their eyes when they heard his story, the fact is that most people who are taken hostage are simply in the wrong place at the wrong time. If, for example, Sam's local fixer in Qamishli had come to the hotel to meet him, instead of arranging to meet at a restaurant down the street, right now you might simply be reading a lighthearted memoir about a young American who traveled to every country in the world.

We wanted the world to see Sam as he was—a bridge-builder between communities, someone who went out into the world to make friends, to learn new things, and to show people in other countries who may have been distrustful of Uncle Sam that most Americans are good, kind, honest people. This is what Sam is. If he were a movie character, he would most likely be played by someone like Jimmy Stewart.

This is a very emotive issue not only for families but also for the population at large. As we saw in the case of Brittney Griner, some people were angry that a deal was cut to essentially do a prisoner swap for Viktor Bout, the notorious Russian arms dealer. Others were upset that Griner was released and not Paul Whelan, a former U.S. Marine accused of spying and sentenced to sixteen years in a Russian prison. I was not involved in Whelan's case, but I do know that when dealing with hostile governments, the United States often has limited room for maneuver.

Different presidents deal with hostage situations in very different ways. Trump prided himself on making deals and brought home an estimated fifty Americans who had been held abroad, including a Mormon missionary who had been held in Venezuela and Bryan Nerren, a pastor who was jailed in India for not declaring $40,000 in cash when entering the country.

It was Thomas Jefferson who had to deal with some of the newly created country's first hostage crises. After the War of Independence, America lacked the powerful protection of the Royal Navy. As a result, the government turned to the old European trick of paying protection money to ward off attacks from Mediterranean pirates based in quasi-city-states in ports stretching across Libya,

My first hockey team, at age five. Bowling Green, Ohio | 1993.

the Dharavi Slum building a human pyramid with a group of local kids, one of countless cherished memories from my travels. Mumbai, India July 28, 2013.

Stephanie Hajjar and Steph Goodwin, while roommates in college, about to leave their apartment for Steph's twenty-second birthday dinner. Nashville, Tennessee | November 21, 2015.

Rob and I with Song Gun Kim, the captain of the North Korean National Hockey Team. We spent a week coaching the local players. Pyongyang, North Korea | March 9, 2016.

With Joss at the airport discussing our previous and upcoming travels. Nadi, Fiji | May 2, 2019.

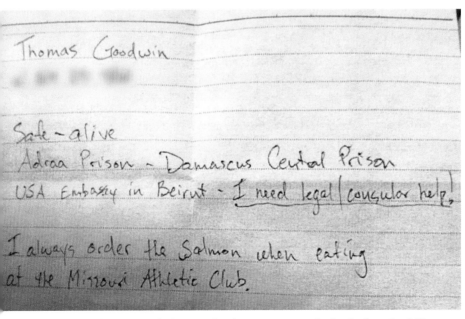

Thomas Goodwin

Safe - alive
Adraa Prison - Damascus Central Prison
USA Embassy in Beirut - I need legal/consular help!

I always order the Salmon when eating at the Missouri Athletic Club.

ne "salmon note" I smuggled out of Adra Prison with the help of a fellow mate. St. Louis, Missouri | June 30, 2019.

The first photo taken with my parents after being freed. Beirut, Lebanon | July 26, 2019.

With General Abbas Ibrahim and Joseph inside the headquarters of Lebanon's General Security Directorate. Beirut, Lebanon | July 26, 2019.

Praying together with my mom at Saint Charbel monastery a few hours following my release. Byblos, Lebanon | July 26, 2019.

With Georgio outside of Saint Charbel monastery. After this photo was taken, Georgio told us the story of his own miracle. Byblos, Lebanon | July 26, 2019.

As a homecoming gesture, my aunt Christi arranged luminaries around the front yard of my parents' house. St. Louis, Missouri | July 27, 2019.

Our family at 11 a.m. Mass at St. Clement. I am still wearing the glasses given to me, and paid for, by the inmates at Adra. St. Louis, Missouri | July 28, 2019.

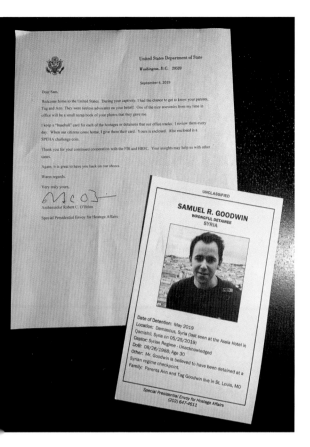

Ambassador Robert O'Brien, the US government's SPEHA in 2019, gave me this letter along with the "baseball card" from my case.
Washington, DC | September 4, 2019.

Steph and I with Luke Hartig, David Bradley, and Emily Lenzner, thanking them for all they did to help bring me home.
Washington, DC | September 10, 2019.

At the base of the Christ the Redeemer statue. Brazil was the final nation on my travel journey to every country in the world. Rio de Janeiro, Brazil | January 1, 2020.

Tim McAtee and Father Vigoa meeting in person for the first time, after being on countless Team SG23 conference calls together in 2019, at the annual Foley Foundation gala dinner. Washington, DC | August 19, 2021.

Sharing my story and message via a keynote presentation at a conference. Arlington, Virginia | October 22, 2023.

Tunisia, and Algeria. At the time, around 15 percent of the United States' overseas trading went through the Mediterranean, so it was an important sea route. When he became the republic's third president, Jefferson decided to stop the payments, prompting the Barbary corsairs to capture US ships and hold their crews and passengers hostage.

In 1801, Jefferson sent a small flotilla to deal with the pirates and free the Americans, but one of the gunships, the USS *Philadelphia*, ran aground near Tripoli. Its crew was captured and marched off to the notorious local slave markets. The captain of one of the US warships, Stephen Decatur, managed to destroy the captured ship. There followed negotiations to try to get the Americans back. When those failed, Jefferson sent a force of Marines under Revolutionary War hero William Eaton to Alexandria in Egypt, where they recruited an additional four hundred local troops. Together, they marched five hundred miles across the blazing desert and stormed the fortified city of Derna, capturing the city and refusing to return it to the leader of Tripoli, Yusuf Qaramanli, until he surrendered his American prisoners.

At the same time, Jefferson, a very practical tactician, had also sent another envoy to Tripoli to offer a financial incentive. The fact that the Marines held Derna gave them extra leverage, but the US government still had to pay $60,000 to free its citizens. It was the first time American troops had captured foreign soil and gave rise to the line, "From the halls of Montezuma to the shores of Tripoli" in the Marine Corps hymn.

Historian Michael Oren even argues that the hostage-taking and ransom payments that haunted US shipping in the Mediterranean in the early days of the republic actually contributed to the drafting of the Constitution. The practice had dogged European shipping since the twelfth century, and countless ships had been seized and hundreds of thousands of people held hostage or sold into slavery, including Miguel de Cervantes, the author of *Don Quixote*. If their captors could extort a ransom, they would release the prisoners. Otherwise, the captives were sold into drudgery in mines or as galley slaves. Some even converted to Islam and took to piracy themselves.

Lacking a functioning navy capable of countering the pirate fleets, US politicians were given an extreme impetus in the 1780s to forge a closer union among the newly independent states than was afforded by the Articles of Confederation. It was the new Constitution that would provide the legal and financial basis for the expensive venture of building a real navy.

Another hostage crisis, this time in Iran in 1979, also played a major role in US politics. When religious revolutionaries who had recently taken power in Tehran stormed the local US embassy, it triggered a 444-day crisis in an election year that pitted incumbent Democratic president Jimmy Carter against Republican California governor Ronald Reagan. With pressure mounting on Carter as the standoff dragged on, and with fifty-two Americans held by the volatile Iranian revolutionaries, Carter launched a daring rescue raid that at the last minute went horribly wrong when a helicopter collided with a jet plane. Eight servicemembers died. The tragedy is widely believed to have cost Carter the election.

Reagan would later be plagued by his own hostage crisis. Hezbollah, the Iranian-backed militia group fighting the Israelis in Lebanon's wars, captured a number of Americans in the 1980s. When Iran secretly asked his administration to break the embargo on selling the Islamic Republic weapons in return for freeing the hostages, Reagan agreed. The proceeds from those sales went to fund far-right guerrillas fighting a bloody campaign against the Marxist government in Nicaragua. When news of the Iran-Contra deal broke, it shook the Reagan presidency to its core and almost cost the president his job.

The stakes for these situations can be extremely high. David Bradley and I discussed all of this with Ann and TAG, looking at strategies they could use to highlight Sam's plight as an abducted traveler. We thought that going public could increase pressure on the administration to act more forcefully on his behalf. Exactly a year before Sam's disappearance, President Trump had appointed Robert O'Brien as SPEHA, and he had secured the release of Andrew Brunson, a pastor who was accused by Turkey of supporting a banned opposition leader, Fethullah Gülen. O'Brien would later successfully pressure Sweden to free US rapper A$AP Rocky, who was on trial for assault after an altercation near a nightclub in Stockholm.

Trump had fired fifty-nine Tomahawk missiles at Syrian military targets two years earlier, in response to a Syrian regime airstrike that dropped sarin nerve gas on the small rebel-held town of Khan Sheikhoun in the northwest, an attack that killed at least eighty people and wounded hundreds more. But as we saw in the case of Jefferson and the Barbary corsairs two hundred years before, sometimes the combination of military force and diplomacy can open up a rival to negotiations.

In the end, the Goodwins decided to wait. The FBI had explicitly warned them not to go public, and we admitted that it came with some risks. Of course, once a case is made public, it can't be made unpublic. This is always a fraught decision to make—your child's life may depend on it, after all—and it also ratchets up the pressure on the family members, who can then become entangled in the relentless glare of media attention.

For now, we decided to focus on building out TAG's network of connections, inching our way closer and closer to Assad's inner core of advisers.

SAM GOODWIN

Every day, in the morning and evening, the terrifying routine of cell doors being slammed and inmates being frantically thrashed was repeated. I could hear the approaching horror, the screams, and the doors creaking open and shut, and I would wonder if this time it was my turn to be beaten to a pulp.

Each time, the big man in the military uniform would stand in my doorway, stare at me, then walk on to torture my neighbor. I had no idea if this was a scare tactic to soften me up, or whether the Syrians genuinely didn't know what to do with me. If the former, it certainly worked. I was terrified every time it happened. Just as bad was the idea that they might be deliberately torturing all these people as a way of getting to me, thinking I was someone important who had to be persuaded to confess to spying or some other crime, at the expense of so many others being brutally attacked.

It was impossible to gauge any of this from "Soleimani," as I thought of him, when he would enter my cell and stare at me. His face was always expressionless, like a mask. He was just doing his job, destroying people.

This, I learned, is what Branch 215 is: a place to destroy human beings. From the street outside, most people wouldn't even know there's a prison down there in the basement. A casual passerby might think the building housed a school, or maybe even a hotel. The regime didn't want the outside world to know what was going on in its torture chambers.

Branch 215 is run by Syria's Military Intelligence Directorate. When protests broke out against the regime in March 2011, in the early days of the Arab Spring, demonstrators were snatched off the streets and from their homes and brought here to face torture and murder. That earned this prison the name among ordinary Syrians: the "Branch of Death."

Much of what we now know about Branch 215 and other torture centers comes from the few people who survived and managed to escape from them, and from a handful of defectors who fled the country. One of the most prominent defectors is a military photographer whose grim task it was to document the bodies of people who had been tortured to death or executed in jail. The man, known for security reasons only as Caesar, smuggled out nearly fifty-five thousand photos of more than eleven thousand people who had been brutally murdered by Assad's thugs. It's estimated that more than thirty-five hundred of them were slaughtered in Branch 215.

Assad has personally denied the evidence, but Human Rights Watch and the FBI have managed to verify that the pictures are in fact real. For additional perspective, the photos only cover the period from March 2011 to August 2013 and are only from a few prisons in the Damascus area. The war and the killing have continued since that time across the entire country. There were so many bodies stacking up that the morgues at military hospitals overflowed, and an open-air garage had to be used to process the dead. It is an ongoing massive crime against humanity, one that remains widely unchecked to this day.

The bodies that Caesar photographed were all meticulously numbered so the regime could keep track of its bloody work. Each one had a number written either on the flesh in pen or on a piece of paper placed on the cadaver. Forensic examinations showed the victims had been bludgeoned to death, starved, suffocated, or shot. Many showed marks of torture and emaciation. Some may have succumbed to disease, given the unsanitary and often overcrowded conditions in the jail, plus the poor diet. Others probably had chronic diseases, such as diabetes or heart conditions, when they were arrested and that were not treated, leading to their deaths.

As in the death camps of Nazi Germany, other inmates were usually tasked with removing and numbering the dead. One of these prisoners charged with writing numbers on the foreheads of the dead was a teenager named Omar Alshogre, with whom I would later become friends in the United States. Omar was just fifteen years old when he was first arrested, attending a peaceful demonstration in his home village of Al-Bayda. The security forces opened fire on the demonstrators, killing Omar's best friend, then detaining him for the first of seven times. The last time he was arrested was when he was visiting his cousins' house in November 2012. An armed militia group loyal to the government burst in and arrested him and three of his cousins, Bashir, Rashad, and Nour. He never found out what happened to Nour, but the three young men—Omar was still only seventeen at the time—were sent to Branch 215. There, they were subjected to unspeakable torture, including electric shocks, having their fingernails pulled out, beatings, and being hung from the ceiling by their arms, which were pinned behind their backs, an agonizing ordeal that slowly dislocates the shoulders.

Rashad died after four months of torture and starvation. Bashir, who often shared some of his food rations with weaker cellmates and who always reminded Omar about the wonderful future he would have when he got out, died in Omar's arms almost a year later, as Omar was helping Bashir—weakened by hunger and torture and suffering from tuberculosis—to the toilet. Omar then had to take his beloved cousin's body to the morgue and mark his forehead with a number.

Omar was in Branch 215 for almost two years. He was then transferred to a place even more notorious for murder and torture—Sednaya Prison. There, he witnessed horrors almost beyond description, something he said he had only seen later on the popular show *Squid Game*, where desperate people are forced to kill one another for a cash prize. He said the guards came into his cell and asked a friend of his who his best friend was. Fortunately for Omar, the chosen prisoner gave the name of another man in the cell, perhaps intuiting that nothing good would come of it. The guards then gave him a screwdriver and calmly ordered him to kill the other prisoner with it, or else they would switch roles and he would be killed. He was given ten minutes to carry out this horrific order. The two men, who really were friends, argued about whose family would be more affected. In the end, the man carried out his orders.

Omar was so badly malnourished and weakened by torture that at one point he collapsed and the guards assumed he was dead. They tossed him into what passed as a morgue—a room filled with abandoned corpses waiting to be picked up and either burned or dumped in mass graves. Omar awoke with a dead man's arm across his face. The man's eyes were still wide open. He dragged himself to the door and banged it until someone opened it up.

"What are you doing in there?" asked the guard.

"I'm alive," Omar said.

The guard looked at him and shrugged. "Why?" he said.

Omar was returned to his cell, where he clung to life for another year before his mother paid a $20,000 bribe to have him smuggled out. When the man who had promised to get him out left the prison, he called Omar's mother on a FaceTime call to confirm that the deed was done. At first, his own mother didn't even recognize her son.

Omar eventually escaped to Sweden with his mother and younger brother. There, he learned that his father and two of his brothers had been killed in a massacre in his own village. Eventually, he made it to Washington, DC, where he enrolled at Georgetown University and today advocates for Syrian refugees and detainees.

Having now reached the three-week mark of sitting alone in Branch 215, the terror swirled around me. All I could hear in my own cell was the screaming of other inmates. I would see the face of the man who loomed in my doorway every morning, threatening to drag me off into this hellscape. I was stuck in the dungeon, plagued by the realization that I was in an environment where nothing was off-limits.

TAG GOODWIN

After about two weeks, I began referring to the Fusion Cell as the "Confusion Cell." Not that they were bad people, but they just didn't seem to be capable of achieving anything. Or at least, nothing they were willing to share with us.

During our first meeting with the FBI at my office in St. Louis, it seemed clear that their main concern was to ensure that a young American hadn't run off to join ISIS. They were pleasant with us when we later met at the Hoover Building in DC, but it seemed as though this was because they really didn't have anything concrete to offer about Sam's case.

They did give us a special manual, a guide that provides an overview of how the Fusion Cell works and includes resources that families can use to help them through an ordeal like this. It was quite bulky, so they suggested that instead of us lugging it around to the other various meetings we had lined up in DC, they would mail it to us. Well, we never got it, and we later learned that they had sent it to the wrong address. It was just a casual bureaucratic slipup, but it did make us wonder: If the FBI couldn't even find our house in St. Louis, how were they going to find our son in Syria?

On top of this, a few weeks after Sam's disappearance, Tim McAtee indicated during a Team SG23 conference call that he could arrange for one of his contacts to go to the Asia Hotel in Qamishli and retrieve Sam's North Face backpack. He said that his International Medical Corps colleague Patrick, who covered security in Syria for the organization, was based in Kobane and frequently traveled to Qamishli. Patrick told Tim that he even knew the folks at the Asia Hotel and could swing by to pick up the bag.

We discussed this move as a team. Would it look suspicious to the Syrians if they learned that Sam's bag was suddenly collected from Qamishli? On the other hand, maybe we should let the Syrians know about the bag since everything in it would attest to the true nature of Sam's travels. In the end, we decided to give Tim and Patrick the green light.

That evening, Ann wrote a short update email to the Fusion Cell, which included a bullet point about us arranging for Sam's bag to be fetched from Qamishli. Moments after she hit send, a representative from the Fusion Call called Ann on the phone. The official disclosed that the US government had already retrieved Sam's bag. Although we were happy to learn that the bag had been found, this was infuriating news. First, why did they not tell us they had the bag? And second, we had been told by them that the US government didn't have any assets on the ground in Syria. This episode confirmed that they were withholding information, for no apparent reason, and it was resulting in us wasting precious time.

Nevertheless, I continued documenting all of my meetings and sharing the information with Paul Osborne, who was now our official FBI case officer. I was documenting everything anyway, just to keep my expanding network in order and to know who was saying what. Most days, I sent a comprehensive update message to Team SG23, laying out the various people we had talked to and noting any promising leads.

Much more encouraging than the FBI was our meeting in mid-June in DC with David Bradley. This was arranged by Luke and Emily, who worked for him. David is a renowned entrepreneur and is always looking for the latest innovations and new ways of doing things. In addition to his handful of thriving businesses, David works—pretty much in his spare time—to help any families whose relatives have been taken by hostile regimes or terror groups.

As a prominent businessman and media figure, he has fantastic contacts. He and Luke presented Ann and me with a diagram they had created outlining the inner circles of Assad's regime and how it expanded outward to merge with the world at large. David said he knew a former US presidential aide now working as a lawyer who had informal contact with Rami Makhlouf, Assad's cousin and Syria's leading business tycoon. He also had suggestions for approaching relatives of Syria's first lady, Asma, who was born in London. In addition, he knew exactly who he wanted to write a profile of Sam for the *New York Times* should we decide to go down that route, portraying Sam as an innocent traveler who just wanted to better understand the world, not spy on foreign governments.

He was sympathetic to our reluctance to go public too quickly. It was true that even if the *Times* published a story, once it was out, we could lose control of the narrative as other papers picked it up. We decided to wait and continue pursuing the back-channel approach. David did caution me that he knew of no Americans who had been released by the Syrian government through the intervention of an NGO or the church. "I wouldn't stay in this lane too long if there are no promising developments." Overall, in that meeting, David graciously made us feel as if we were the most important people in the world.

David's efficiency only highlighted the clay-footedness of the government. I would send the Fusion Cell good leads every day and not hear a word back from them. When I followed up, they would say, "Oh yeah, we haven't gotten to it yet." It became clear they either weren't going to, or they weren't going to tell me what they were doing. This one-way communication made me feel as if we were on opposing teams and as if I was working with one arm tied behind my back. It seemed virtually impossible to productively collaborate with them. On a few rare occasions, they called and asked us to drive over to the FBI field office in downtown St. Louis. This happened when they apparently had sensitive material to share and wanted to do it within the security of their own building.

I went to one of these meetings, and afterward decided never to go again. They had called us on very short notice and said they had information to share. Of course, we dropped everything and rushed over. Thankfully, on the way, one of the local, on-the-ball agents took the trouble to call us and warn us not to get our hopes up. He had enough empathy to know how keen we'd be to find out something meaningful from the FBI, but he'd already seen the information they were going to deliver and knew it was far from significant.

They took us into one of their secure rooms and loaded a video.

It was security camera footage from a street in Qamishli, showing Sam walking through the market area just before he was kidnapped. There were four snippets of video, all clearly from cameras mounted on adjacent lampposts, and the clips ran sequentially. It was clearly Sam, but it stopped right at the moment he was about to call Ann on FaceTime, the moment he was grabbed. We asked if we could see the next one. After all, if they had the moments before the disappearance, they surely must have the moment itself.

"No," they said. "That's where it stops. We don't have any more."

"Yes, you do," insisted Ann. But they swore that they didn't have any more. It seemed clear to us they were concealing something vital, for reasons we couldn't fathom. But there wasn't anything more we could do. They told us we could have copies of the video later, after it was declassified. Despite several inquiries, to this day, we've not received anything.

One evening, as I was walking into the Missouri Athletic Club to work out, Paul, the case officer, called me. Paul had previously been on security detail for government staff and visiting dignitaries, so it was fairly clear that running investigations and dealing with stressed families wasn't really his thing. His phone call was to return a message I had left him earlier in the day asking if he'd had a chance to follow up on some information I'd sent him.

He hadn't, and the phone call was just hot air, wasting my own valuable time. I lost it on him right there in the parking lot.

"Paul, all you guys are doing is slowing us down. You're creating more work for me. Paul, I am done. I did everything you guys wanted, and I don't think we're going to follow your direction anymore. You wanted us to keep this on the down-low, well, I think I'm gonna go public." I wasn't actually thinking of doing this, but he had just made me so angry.

He responded by telling me I shouldn't do that and that it would be a disaster. Interestingly, in a soft and almost defeated voice, he admitted to me that the FBI has its challenges and has opportunity for improvement.

When I got home late that night, I vented to Ann. "We're not working with the Fusion Cell anymore. We're done with them."

Ann was alarmed. "No, no, no," she said. "We're not cutting them off like that."

After a minute or so, I relented. Of course, she was right, but personally, I was done with them. "Fine, if you want to communicate with them, that's your responsibility. But I'm not having anything more to do with the Confusion Cell."

STEPHANIE (STEPH) GOODWIN

For some reason, afternoons were always hard for me. I would usually wake up early in the morning and supercharge my day with a run or a session at the gym and then throw myself into my real estate work to try to stop my brain from spinning in circles. By the early afternoon, though, my mind and body would slow down and I'd start to dwell on what was happening to Sam and whether I'd ever see my brother again.

I had pretty much stopped seeing other friends and going out to gatherings. Being laser focused on just one thing that I couldn't talk about made me not great company. There was no way I could act normal around people all the time when the worst thing in my life was happening. It was like low-grade depression. I couldn't concentrate on anything else so I didn't really want to see anyone, even though I knew that being with my friends could potentially help my disposition.

Within our immediate family, no one ever missed anyone else's phone calls. If my dad called one of us, we picked up on the first ring, always half expecting bad news. Instead, there was usually no news, week after week. Every day, I'd speak to Betty and Mom, just to let some steam out of the pressure valve of anxiety in our heads, trying not to lose our faith.

On the afternoon of Friday, June 14, three weeks since Sam had disappeared, I was feeling a bit restless, sticky, and anxious. Betty was in Portugal walking the Camino, making it a bit more challenging to reach her to talk. It was hot outside, at least 85 degrees, and I decided to go for a run to blow off some steam.

Just as I was about to head out, for some reason my old college roommate from Belmont University popped into my head. I hadn't seen Stephanie Hajjar since the previous Christmas, when I'd gone to visit her and her family in Scottsdale, Arizona. Stephanie was now living in Los Angeles, working as an emotional wellness coach for entertainers, athletes, and musicians. A lot of her work dealt with teenage actors struggling with the pressures of fame and money. Slightly different issues than having your brother kidnapped by a genocidal regime, but still, I knew she'd be willing to listen and might be able to offer some much-needed advice on how to cope with extreme stress. Despite the US government continuing to tell us to keep our communication circles very tight, I decided to call Stephanie.

I dialed her number. No answer. She must be busy. I went out for the jog, hammering the streets of Nashville until I was soaked in sweat. When I got home, I had a text message from Stephanie. She was at a bridal shower in Texas. She asked if everything was okay and if she could call me back later. I replied, "No and yes." The phone rang a few minutes later.

I didn't beat around the bush. "Things are literally horrible. You are not going to believe what I'm going to tell you, but my brother went missing in Syria and no one has heard from him in three weeks," I blurted out before she could really say anything.

"Oh my gosh," she said, dumbfounded. Of all the people I could have told, Stephanie was the most likely to grasp the gravity of the situation. Unbeknownst to me, her Maronite Catholic family came from Lebanon during the civil war in the 1980s and had settled in the Southwest of the United States.

"That is not good," she said, clearly trying to play down how awful she knew it really was.

I launched into an explanation of the insane search with the FBI and the CIA, the Vatican, the Russians, and the special forces on standby to launch a million-dollar raid. "This is going to end so badly. No one can even tell us where he is," I said.

Stephanie listened in shocked silence as I poured out my sorry tale.

"Oh my gosh," she said at last. "Is there anything I can do?"

"Well," I said, "from what I understand, unless you know someone who is friends with Assad, all you can do is pray."

There was a pause, and then Stephanie replied, "Wait, let me call you back."

Stephanie is one of the most rock-solid people I know, and she is not the sort who would promise something she couldn't deliver. So as I hung up the phone, I thought, "Wait, what the heck..."

STEPHANIE HAJJAR, *25, Steph Goodwin's*
former college roommate

My father came to visit the United States in 1988. His family had been trying to escape from Lebanon for years, primarily because the country had been torn apart by a civil war. Sectarian factionalism pitted the various Muslim groups against one another and against the Christian Maronites.

While he was in the US, his family called and told him not to come back because the war was getting so bad. They then joined him a couple of years later. I was born and raised in Texas, and even though I grew up in the rich culture of my Lebanese heritage, I have unfortunately not yet visited the country.

Steph and I became friends on our first day of college at Belmont University in Nashville in 2012. I was going to a freshman orientation event, waiting in line to enter the building, when someone behind me tapped me on the shoulder.

"Hi," the girl said. "I'm Steph."

"What a coincidence," I said, glad to meet a new friend. "So am I!"

We started chatting and found we had a lot in common, including the fact that we had both gone to all-girls Catholic high schools. We decided then and there to go to Mass together on Sunday, and that was the start of a long and fulfilling friendship. In our junior year, we became roommates and lived together for the next two years. Even after we both graduated from Belmont and I moved to Los Angeles and she went off to join Sam at his company in Singapore, we kept in regular touch.

I studied music business at school and audited a class on emotional intelligence in the entertainment industry, taught by an emotional wellness coach for entertainers. It was then that I knew what I wanted to pursue for my career. This career path combined a number of things I loved—helping people, health and wellness, and the entertainment business. The course blew my mind and the professor became my mentor. When I graduated, I moved to Los Angeles to start working as an emotional wellness and mental performance coach, helping athletes, musicians, and actors manage the stress of the business and the pressures of being a public personality. A lot of the work I do is helping young entertainment professionals navigate life in the limelight and simultaneously achieve the level of health and success they desire.

The last time I'd spoken to Steph had been about a month before, when she had called to tell me she just got engaged. I was very excited for her, so when I got a text message saying things weren't good, I automatically assumed that an issue had arisen with her fiancé. I was at a bridal shower for a childhood friend in Texas, so I went upstairs to find a quiet room where I could talk to her privately and offer whatever support she might need. Mentally, I began cursing her fiancé, Matt.

When she told me her brother had gone missing in Syria, I was in sheer disbelief. I'd never been there, but because of my family background, I knew more about the horrors of the Assad regime than most Americans. Steph vaguely knew I was of Lebanese descent but admitted to me she hadn't actually known where Lebanon was, or that it was right next to Syria. I listened to her as she recounted in a somber voice how Sam appeared to have fallen off the face of the planet, and I knew this was devastating news. But our family has a lot of Syrian friends, so I was sure someone knew someone who could help. Traditionally, there is a lot of cross-pollination between tiny Lebanon and its larger neighbor, and many Lebanese have friends or relatives in Syria. These days, Lebanon is also full of desperate refugees from Syria's war who are struggling to survive as Lebanon suffers its own massive economic crash.

"What can I do to help?" I asked Steph, once she had told me her shocking tale.

She clearly didn't expect any practical help, so I said I would certainly pray for her and be there to support her emotionally. But the whole time, I was thinking that I could potentially do something more concrete too.

"Let me call you back," I said.

She sounded very surprised, but I hung up and went through the house to find my dad, who was also there for the party. As I was walking, I shot Steph a quick text asking if it was okay to tell my dad, in strictest confidence. She went and asked her own father, who quickly agreed. When I found my dad, I asked him to come upstairs so our conversation wouldn't be overheard by anyone.

He was profoundly shocked when I told him about Sam. I asked him how bad it was. "This is *so* bad," he said. Then he added, "Why is he in Syria? You know how if someone tries to come to the United States and is accused of spying, the authorities will detain that person and send them back to their own country? Well, in Syria, it's a hundred times worse."

"Do you think Uncle Joseph would know somebody in Lebanon who could help?" I asked.

Uncle Joseph is my dad's brother-in-law, who was living in Connecticut at that time. He'd been an officer in the Lebanese Army, and I thought he still might have some government or security contacts there. In fact, Joseph would sometimes remind us that he had served in the armed forces with Michel Aoun, who had been the commander of the Lebanese Army at the time and went on to be elected Lebanon's president in 2016. That had to count for *something*, I figured.

After we talked, I texted Steph again. "Can my dad talk to your dad?" A few minutes later, we received a message back saying yes.

My dad called TAG, and in that initial conversation, he felt it was best to play his cards close to his chest. He said that with TAG's permission, he would ask his brother-in-law Joseph in Connecticut to make some discreet inquiries. TAG gave him his permission, so then my dad called Uncle Joseph.

Joseph immediately agreed to try to help and told us he would get back to us after he had made some calls.

SAM GOODWIN

A few hours after I'd faked my last hyperventilation attack—and narrowly avoided having a not-too-clean hypodermic needle plunged into my vein—some unusual things began to happen in the dungeon. In the evening of day 23, a guard came to my cell and said, "*Hammam*," which I had learned meant "shower." I could tell from my tiny scrap of window that it was only about seven in the evening. Up to this point, I had never had a shower before ten or eleven at night.

A different guard walked me back to my cell afterward, and as he closed the door, he said, "*Ingiliiziyya al-yawma*," which I determined meant "English today." "Somebody's going to talk to me in English today?" I asked. He nodded, then slammed the door.

Ten minutes later, another guard came and handed me a brand-new box of Syrian cookies. I accepted them and gratefully ate them, the first sweet thing I'd eaten in almost a month. A few minutes later, a guard opened the door and handed me a bottle of orange soda. This too was unprecedented. I'd had nothing but water since I'd been detained. Not to mention that this all constituted more activity in the space of half an hour than I'd had in the previous week.

Clearly, something was going on, but I had no way of knowing what it was and whether it might be the start of something good or much, much worse. Was this a parting gift before my release, or a last meal before I was executed? Was I about to be tortured, or would I be seeing the prison boss and the guards wanted me to speak well of them?

It was about nine o'clock when the door opened again. Two guards came in and told me to follow them. They marched me to the foot of the stairs leading out of the basement, then we halted. One of them hand-cuffed my hands behind my back while the other blindfolded me with a black cloth. They then guided me up the stairs to the street level of the prison. It was the first time I had left the basement dungeon in more than three weeks.

At the top of the steps, we entered a room and they sat me down in a chair. I had no idea if I was alone in the room or if there was someone in there with me. Then a man started speaking from across the room.

"Hi, Sam," he said, in perfect, American-accented English.

For weeks, I'd been desperate to speak to anyone in English. I'd begged my guards to get me in front of an English speaker so I could tell them the truth about who I was. Now I was so nervous—hands cuffed behind my back, blinded by the cloth around my eyes—that my throat was so dry I could barely get any words out. Being hand-cuffed and blindfolded at the same time is physically and psycholog-ically an incredibly vulnerable position to be in. I had no idea who this man was and if he might be standing next to me with a pistol to my head.

The interrogator then started asking me about every aspect of my life, beginning on August 26, 1988, the day I was born, and work-ing all the way up to the present day. I answered him truthfully and respectfully, always addressing him as "sir." Every so often he would translate my answers into Arabic for some other people who were also clearly in the room. I never saw anyone, but I could hear them muttering in response to his translations, along with the occasional creak of their chairs on the floor.

It was surreal how much this man wanted to know, right down

to how my dad takes his coffee, the occupation of my sister's fiancé, everything imaginable. He of course asked about why I came to Syria. I told him I was on a quest to travel to every country in the world and that Syria was 181 of 193. I had twelve left to visit.

Then, about an hour into the interrogation, he said, "Sam, don't read too much into this question, but what religion are you?" I told him I practice Christianity. "I'm Catholic." He replied, "Oh, there are a lot of Catholics in Syria."

I'm not sure how I knew this—just one of the many weird travel facts I had picked up on my journeys—but I told him, "Yes, before the current Pope Francis, the last non-European pope was from Syria." I recall this being the only time I spoke out of turn.

He replied, "Oh yes, that's right. I did know that." This proved to be among the most tolerant moments of the entire interrogation.

There were some other surreal comments. The man, whose face I never saw, asked me what I'd had in my bag in the hotel in Qamishli. I said I had my phone and my computer.

"What computer?" he asked. I told him it was a MacBook Pro, and he said, conversationally, "Oh, I'm thinking of getting a new one. Do you like it?" It was hard for me to tell—especially after not having spoken to a living soul in weeks—if these were genuine moments of connection or the tricks of a professional interrogator in whose hands my life now rested.

After about two and a half hours of this probing, he said, "Okay, Sam, now let's talk about setting you free. What are your thoughts?"

My heart lifted. This was it. I was getting out. Finally, this whole mistake was going to be corrected.

"Well, sir," I said, "I know the Lebanon border is close by. If you could take me overland there and leave me, I'd be happy to go to Beirut and sort everything else out on my own. Or you could take me to the airport. I have legal residency in the United Arab Emirates, so I could fly directly there, if that helps. I don't think this will work, but if you took me back to Qamishli, I also could exit back to Iraq the same way I came in."

I was positively fizzing with ideas.

But the interrogator responded with, "Okay, Sam, unfortunately we can't do any of those."

My heart began to sink again. From there, he proceeded to tell me the three things that he could do. And that's where it all started to fall apart again.

"Sam, the first thing I can do is to hand you over to Russian forces."

I paused. "Okay, sir, what would they do with me?" At the time, I was modestly familiar with Russia's support of the Syrian regime. The man's emphasis on the word *forces*, rather than diplomats, was unsettling. I had played hockey with many Russians over the years and therefore had plenty of Russian friends, but it didn't seem like that was going to help me here.

"I'm not sure, you'd have to figure it out with them," he said.

"Okay," I said. "What's the next option?"

"I can hand you over to SIA. The Syrian International Authorities."

I had never heard of this organization and had no idea who they were. Much later, I would discover that *nobody* has ever heard of them. They appear to be a fictional invention.

"And what would they do with me?"

"I'm not sure, but they'd probably hold you in a cell until the US embassy reopens in Damascus," he said.

The US embassy had been closed for about seven years by this point, and there was no sign it would ever reopen under the current regime.

"What's option number three?" I asked, feeling a queasiness in the pit of my stomach.

"You can exit overland to Turkey, the Golan Heights, or Jordan, but you need to go by smuggler."

This made no sense to me. Why would they propose that I smuggle my way out of the country? Especially when it would be so easy for me to just show up at any of these borders and walk across with my American passport. I was pretty sure anyone trying to sneak across the border at three in the morning under the cover of darkness would be shot, especially if that border was with Israel—where the Golan Heights are currently located—a country that is still officially at war with Syria and which often carries out bombing raids against Iranian forces operating there.

"Sir, there have to be some other options." I proceeded to ask if he could hand me over to the Catholic Church, or even if he could put me on a cargo ship to somewhere, literally anywhere.

"Sam," he said, "these are the three options. Tell me which one you want. Tell me right now."

At this point, my face was dripping with sweat under the blindfold, my eyes stinging from the salt. My shoulders were in agony from being twisted back by the handcuffs for almost three hours, and my wrists were chafed by the metal. Now this guy was asking me to make one of the most critical decisions of my life, in isolation and with limited information, right here and now.

I decided to be direct. "Sir, I am desperate to get out of this prison. But I can't choose one of those options."

"Okay, Sam," he said. "It's late. Let's wrap this up and we'll pick it up again tomorrow."

And that was it. I was led back downstairs to the dungeon. I was uncuffed. The guards showed an unusual curiosity about how the interrogation had gone, using thumb gestures and basic Arabic and English words to inquire.

"Not very good," I said. As I was escorted back into my cell, I had one of the most ironic thoughts of my life. "I think I'd prefer to just stay in this cell." This cell was seemingly better than getting involved with Russian forces, SIA, or smugglers. It was midnight but there was no way I could sleep. I took my chip of rock and started writing out my choices on the cell door, with lines pointing to pros and cons.

Two of them—the smuggling route and the Russians—could potentially lead to my liberation. But they could also be traps to get me killed and blame someone else. The Syrian regime could simply see this as a way to dispose of my body with plausible deniability. The third, the shadowy SIA, sounded like an indefinite prison term. There was no way the United States was ever going to reopen its embassy with this genocidal regime in power, and the regime had now been shored up by the Russian intervention to last potentially for decades. It made me wonder if any other previously vanished Americans had been offered these same options and if they had said yes to any of them.

There was no way I could accept any of these three choices. I later learned that this three-option game was a total scam by Syrian intelligence just to see how I would react, but at the time, it seemed like life or death to me and I treated it as such. Having arrived at the decision to hold off on choosing one of these options, I was able to eventually fall asleep.

STEPHANIE (STEPH) GOODWIN

Dad had sounded almost annoyed that Friday afternoon when I called him at his office where he was working, both at his day job and building out his network to find Sam. He was a bit brusque and said something like, "I have so much to do right now. What do you need?"

"Dad, I know this might sound crazy, but do you remember my roommate Stephanie Hajjar? I roomed with her in college."

"Yeah," he said, still gruff. "Why do you ask?"

"I just told her about Sam and she said her dad wants to call you. I don't know if he can help, but I know they're Lebanese and I know they're quite well connected in that part of the world. Maybe it's something?"

"Okay, have him call me," he said. So I texted Stephanie back, and our dads then spoke to each other for a while. Afterward, Dad told me that Stephanie's uncle in Connecticut had some good contacts who he felt might be able to help, but beyond that, he didn't know anything.

The following Sunday morning, I got a call from Dad. I was sitting in a coffee shop in Nashville, getting some work done. He cut to the chase. George, Stephanie Hajjar's dad, had called.

"You won't believe it," George had told Dad. "We just received confirmation from Joseph's 'friend' that Sam is safe, alive, and in prison in Damascus!"

Of course, Dad had pressed him for more. After all, this was potentially momentous news. But George wouldn't say any more, and in fact he asked that Dad and I not tell anyone who our Lebanese contact was. His brother-in-law Joseph refused to tell them who his contact was, nor did he want anyone to know that he was in any way involved. Reluctantly, Dad agreed. From this point forward, when he talked about this Lebanon channel, he always referred to it simply as "Joe from Connecticut."

Needless to say, this was wild news. But since there was nothing to back it up, it was also tantalizingly vague. After all, it had been weeks and the FBI and the CIA had come up with nothing. Now my college roommate's uncle was saying he knew Sam was alive after just two days? It was hard to believe. I kept calling Stephanie to see what she had heard from her family, but she is an incredibly loyal person, and her family had insisted she share nothing with us. Stephanie wasn't withholding information from me, she just didn't have much to offer except that she trusted her uncle. She would try to console me, saying, "My uncle won't let me down," and "Let's keep praying." If I tried to press her further, she would remind me it was entirely possible our phones were now tapped, either by the FBI or the Syrians or the Lebanese. That in itself brought me some strange comfort, that her connections might be so important that her phone was actually deemed worth tapping. Or it could all be nothing. We just didn't know.

SAM GOODWIN

The next morning, on day 24 of my captivity, I was woken up by one of the guards slamming open the door and barking. I couldn't understand his words, but from his body language I concluded that he was saying something like, "Let's go now!"

I had been sound asleep, having been up half the night fretting over whether I might be about to make a decision that could cost me either my freedom or my life. In a span of about ten seconds, I went from deep sleep to staggering down the corridor, back to the stairs that led up to the interrogation room.

Just like the night before, the minions blindfolded and handcuffed me. This time, however, they cuffed my hands in front of my body, which was a vast improvement. Imagine sitting for hours and not being able to scratch your face or wipe the sweat out of your eyes.

They took me to a different room this time and sat me down in a chair. Then I heard the same voice from the night before.

"Sam, you don't have much time," he began. "You have to answer every question quickly and truthfully, and only speak when I tell you to. Understood?"

I said I understood; then he hit me with his first question. What is your full name?

For the next twenty minutes, he asked pretty much the same questions as the night before. Maybe he was confirming the basics, or maybe there were different people listening now. Or maybe this was all just a mind game designed to throw me even more off balance.

After a while, he said, "Okay, now I want to talk about how you came to Syria. I want every last detail of how you came from Erbil to Qamishli."

I proceeded to tell him even the smallest details, from how much I paid the driver, what currency I paid in, and how the road was, right down to the make of the car, my room number at the Asia Hotel, and the shawarma I had eaten on the street.

"And why? Why did you come here?"

I restrained myself from yelling, "I already told you that a million times!" Instead, I patiently repeated the same information I had communicated the night before and to every Syrian official along the way. I told him again that I was on a journey to travel to every country in the world.

At that, he flared up. "I don't believe you!"

I insisted. "I'm a traveler." And then I actually said to him, "You can look at my blog."

"No, you know you came here for other reasons," he said, his voice rising again. I was alarmed but tried to calmly insist about my intentions.

"I don't know what that means, sir," I said.

"You're a liar!" he snarled. "Stand up! You no longer get to sit."

I was terrified now. I stood up, legs shaking slightly, not knowing if someone might be standing behind me with a gun to my head or an electric baton.

"Sam, you better start telling the truth or I will do a one-eighty with your life. Do you want me to hand you over to ISIS? I'll do it right now!"

"Please, no, sir," I begged.

We stood like that for a moment before he calmed down and turned back to questioning me about Qamishli. Since I had simply stayed at a hotel there and walked down the street, I could freely tell him without the risk of getting anyone in trouble.

After almost three hours like this, he once again said it was time to talk about setting me free. This time, there was no flutter of hope in my stomach, just a wary sense of caution.

"Which Syrian authority would you like me to hand you over to, Sam?"

"Sir, I don't know any Syrian authorities," I said.

"No, just tell me which one and I'll give you to them," he said, in the reasonable but hectoring tone of a schoolyard bully who knows his helpless victim cannot possibly answer the question he is posing.

"Sir, I'm really sorry, I don't know."

"Okay, then, which *American* authority would you like me to contact on your behalf?"

I was skeptical about whether he would actually contact any Americans, but I suggested the State Department.

"What about the FBI?"

"Yeah, they'd probably be good," I said, dutifully playing the game.

"Okay, Sam, which international authority would you like me to hand you over to?"

I suggested the United Nations, or the Red Cross if they had a presence in Syria, as well as the Catholic Church.

This episode of naming various authorities didn't go anywhere, and a few minutes later, the conversation took a turn. The man—whose name I never knew and whose face I never saw—said, "Okay, Sam, now I'm going to name a country and you're going to tell me yes or no if you've been there."

I readily agreed.

The interrogator had prepared a list of 193 countries and proceeded to name every single one of them, in no particular order and with no pattern of geographical grouping. I actually had to help him with the pronunciation of a few of them.

When we got to the end, there was a pause and the interrogator quietly talked in Arabic with someone next to him. I got the sense that his helper was writing or taking notes on my answers. Sounding like someone who was a bit defeated, he said to me, "Yes, Sam, just as you said, exactly twelve remaining."

I had said no precisely twelve times. Had I actually been an American spy, this would have been a smart way to catch me. Admittedly, this was a very clever interrogation tactic. It would have been extremely difficult to remember a cover story where I named exactly the right number of countries out of 193 pulled in random order from a list, knowing that one slipup would undermine my entire story. Interestingly, and fortunately for me it was super easy, because traveling to every country had been my whole life for the past year and I was acutely familiar with the details of the quest.

Following this episode, the entire sentiment of the interrogation became slightly less tense. It seemed as though the Syrians were potentially beginning to believe that I was the person I was saying I was and not an American spy, as they had wrongfully accused. At about the three-hour mark, the interrogator said, "Okay, Sam, let's take a break now, but we have a lot more to talk about." I never spoke to that man again.

The guards were ordered to take me back to my cell. It was midday, and they gave me some food, since I had missed the egg for breakfast. I ate, but I drank as little water as possible, just in case I was taken back for questioning that afternoon. But they didn't come back.

A day passed. Two days. Three. Nothing. During these days, the guards occasionally gave me a look that seemed to question what I was still doing there. Maybe they had been told I was being moved and the cookies and soda had been a parting gift? Perhaps the result of the interrogation was irrelevant and they were going to hold me in this dungeon forever?

On my twenty-seventh day of solitary confinement, the guards took me out of my cell again and led me to the bottom of the steps. I assumed I was about to face another round of questioning, but instead they uncuffed my hands and presented me with a printed document. It was all in Arabic, except for three words in Latin script in the middle of page one—"Samuel Robert Goodwin," my name.

There was no one there to translate the Arabic text or explain to me what it said. One of the guards was holding an inkpad and indicated I should put my thumb in it to sign the incomprehensible document. Another guard was encouraging me to sign, saying, "Good, home, mother," apparently indicating that he believed I was being released.

I flicked through it. There were twelve pages in total. Confession to spying or other crimes? Maybe. Or possibly some legal waiver for whatever they were about to do to me? I didn't believe for a minute it was a release form, after all the times I had been lied to since my kidnapping. But clearly there was no choice. I put my thumb on the inkpad and signed the paper. They made me thumbprint all twelve pages.

I was taken back to my cell, but very soon after that, they came back and led me upstairs. To my surprise, I wasn't handcuffed or blindfolded. As we crossed an industrial-looking covered courtyard, a man approached me with a plastic bag. Inside was my phone, disassembled into its small components and with the SIM card taped to the back of the case, my passport, and my wallet. This did give me some sense of hope. They were handing back my personal belongings. That had to be positive.

Sure enough, they led me outside the prison to a parking lot where a white minivan was waiting. I sat close to the front, where a driver and a guard with a gun were sitting. Then they loaded two men with big beards who clambered to the back of the vehicle, followed by a woman with three children. That was a surprise, that there had been children in the prison, though I had thought I had heard kids' voices occasionally in the cell next to me. I shuddered to think what they might have been through. Their faces were expressionless. I couldn't see the woman's face because she was clad in a black niqab covering everything except her eyes.

The van pulled out, and all of a sudden we were driving through Damascus. I gazed out the window of the vehicle, relatively nervous about what might be happening, and quietly whispered to myself, "Oh my gosh, that's a tree." After a month of seeing nothing but concrete, my eyes and brain had nearly forgotten how to process colors and the sight of another living thing. I was also thinking, "Damn, I always wanted to see Damascus." The streets looked pretty normal, like any other large Middle Eastern city. As we wound our way through the busy streets, I started to allow myself to hope that they might be taking us to Lebanon.

We hadn't gone far when the vehicle pulled up outside a building and I was told to get out. This building turned out to be a police station. Still, it appeared to be a regular police station, with people milling around and lining up at desks and officers in uniform.

They put me in a room with a crowd of other men who were being held. They appeared somewhat confused by my presence, but there was no real interaction, as none of them seemed to speak English. We sat there for about five hours before an officer came in with a square metal box that he set down on the floor and opened. Inside were metal wrist shackles. Without needing to be told, the men all reached in and grabbed one, which they snapped into place around their wrists. One showed me how to do it. A minute later, another official came in with a very long chain. Everyone lined up and each prisoner took the chain from the man in front of him and fed it through his shackles so we were all linked together.

Firmly secured, we were led outside and loaded into the back of a large truck that smelled as if raw meat had recently been hanging in it. I later heard that this ritual was known colloquially among Syrian prisoners as "the slave walk into the meat truck."

The truck was so crowded that we were more like sardines than sides of beef. Thankfully, the journey was short. We soon pulled up to another large prison building and were ordered into a much larger cell than before, me and roughly thirty other men. We stayed here for the next two days. We could lie down to sleep, thank goodness, but it was tightly packed. A couple of prison workers came around with hair clippers to trim our beards. I had a month of growth on my face but never saw what I looked like because there were no mirrors or windows in this world.

That evening, the guards brought in a large barrel of rice and beans and a bag full of bread, which they set in the middle of the cell. I'm sure the men around me must have been ravenous, but they said to me in their halting English, "You eat first, you are our guest. Then we will eat."

In all of my travels, I've found the hospitality in the Middle East to be the best in the world, and it was all the more moving in this jail cell with these men—most of whom were just petty thieves rather than political prisoners, from what I could tell—who were no doubt fearful for their own futures. I had a small bite, not sure how much there would be to go around. That was enough to allow them to dig in too. We all ate together, sitting on the floor. It wasn't the exit from

Syria I'd been hoping for, but it was a significant upgrade from solitary confinement.

FATHER VIGOA

By late June, the search for Sam had become like a high-stakes game of Chutes and Ladders. Although we were intrigued and cautiously optimistic about our new path via Stephanie and the Lebanese, we simultaneously agreed it would be prudent of us to continue quietly pursuing other channels too. There'd been plenty of progress in terms of accessing people through my church networks, but there was also no shortage of disappointments.

A friend of mine at Caritas, an international group of Catholic organizations, had experience in such cases and agreed to approach the Syrian delegation to the United Nations headquarters in New York City. We all traveled to New York for this meeting, and in preparation for it, TAG and Ann drafted a very respectful and carefully worded letter to Syria's UN ambassador, Bashar Jaafari, to soften him up ahead of the meeting.

"Your Excellency Dr. Jaafari, it is with the deepest love of parents for their children that we write to request a meeting with you," they said, explaining the background of Sam's trip, and how he had taught children in poor countries and tried to help build ties between cultures.

"Sam is on a personal pilgrimage to visit every country in the world and experience the beauty that every country has to offer. He was especially excited to visit Syria, the heart of the Arab world and a country of deep historical and religious significance."

We never received a response from the UN delegation. My contact at Caritas told me that "when they heard the word *American*, they became very reluctant to meet Sam's parents."

I also wrote to the nunciature, which is a diplomatic mission or embassy of the Vatican, in Lebanon to see if they could exert any leverage on getting us a meeting with the Syrian ambassador to the Vatican. They wrote back saying it was out of their jurisdiction and that only the Syrian nunciature could assist with that.

I also enlisted the Vatican's own ambassador to the UN, Archbishop Bernardito Auza, a friend of mine, to lean on the Syrians for a meeting. He agreed to meet TAG, Ann, Sam's brother Paul, and myself at the Vatican residence in New York City. Archbishop Auza is from the Philippines, so to help win him over, Ann brought one of her scrapbooks to the meeting, which included a handful of photos of Sam in Tacloban. In 2013, while living in Asia, he had organized disaster relief efforts to help locals recover from the devastation of Typhoon Yolanda. The archbishop was deeply moved by the images.

That same day, I was thrilled to receive an email from a close aide to the patriarch of the Syriac Orthodox Church, Ignatius Ephrem II. I had high hopes for this particular channel. Not only was he the leading prelate of one of the oldest Christian communities in the world—the Church of Antioch had been established in AD 32 by Saint Peter himself—but he was born in Qamishli, the very town where Sam had disappeared. Despite his impressively biblical-sounding title—Patriarch of Antioch and All the

East—Ignatius had spent almost twenty years living in the United States as the archbishop of the American Syriac church for the eastern half of the country, based in Teaneck, New Jersey.

The email I received was forwarded by one of his US-based bishops, Gregory Mansour, and the news was encouraging. "Our bishop in Damascus is following up on Sam's issues," the patriarch told the bishop. "He provided information to the concerned authorities. We are expecting some news about it today such as confirming his whereabouts and conditions. I will pass on the information as soon as I get it. Let's hope for the best."

That seemed to bode well, so we went out to dinner in New York that evening to celebrate. While we were eating, however, I received a disheartening message from Cardinal Zenari, on whom I had been pinning many hopes. A piece of his email read:

Dear Father Richard,

I am in Verona with some health problems. I broke both my arms in a fall. So I do hope to return to Syria in the middle of July. I understand perfectly the suffering of the parents of Sam. Probably somebody betrayed him. The matter as far as I can understand is very delicate and complicated. The USA government has to intervene and Damascus in return will try to obtain what it wants. Let us pray.
                                                            Mons Mario Zenari.

That was a disappointment for sure. I tried to reassure TAG and Ann that we had known from the start that this would be a long haul, and together, we had plenty of other routes to get to Sam.

Little did we know, Sam was also working on his own.

SAM GOODWIN

On the morning of June 22, 2019, having now been locked in Syria for thirty days, I was led outside with other men into a yard to be sorted. Hundreds of men stood chained together for hours as the guards consulted lists and identities and herded us into cages to await the next stage of the journey. When my cage was full and the guards decided they had everyone on their list, we were again loaded into the back of a meat truck and driven across town.

The first place they took us was the so-called Palace of Justice. Still chained together, we were shuffled inside into holding cells in the basement of the building and were taken out one by one over the next several hours. When it was my turn, I was led upstairs to speak in front of a female judge who spoke rudimentary English. She appeared to be a real judge. Even though the courts were seemingly just window dressing for a police state, the bureaucratic rites still had to be observed. So everyone was duly found guilty by actual judges, who acted out of either fear or loyalty, or perhaps just for the paycheck.

She asked me to explain why I came to Syria, then said that they were trying to work with the US embassy in Damascus to figure out what to do with me. By now, I knew this was all just empty talk as the embassy had been shut for years. In the meantime, she said, I would be held in prison.

"How long will that be?" I asked her.

"Maybe nine weeks," she said.

I don't know where she got that figure. Maybe she just made it up, but it was shattering to me. Nine more weeks in solitary. I wasn't sure I would make it through, since my only experience of prison in Syria so far was Branch 215.

That afternoon, when our meat truck set out again, I could see through a small window that we appeared to be heading out of the city. After about half an hour, we stopped outside a prison that wouldn't have looked entirely out of place by the side of a highway in Missouri. The fact that it actually looked like a prison was somehow reassuring, unlike the covert dungeon where I had been hidden away for the past month.

Processing the new arrivals took hours. We sat outside in a yard covered against the sun, waiting to be summoned inside. One of the men in my cohort spoke some English and told me the prison was called Adra. The name meant nothing to me. I asked if we would sleep on the floor, like Branch 215, or in a bed. He said there were beds here, and better food, if you could pay. That was a blow, since I didn't have a penny to my name.

Then we were led inside and given white-and-gray-striped uniforms, like convicts in old American gangster movies. A guard confiscated the small bag of belongings I had been given when I left Branch 215. In it was my broken-down phone, passport, and wallet, while my other belongings had been left in my North Face backpack at the Qamishli hotel. I was confident I would never see that bag again. Clad in prison uniforms, we were marched, unchained, into a crowded dormitory with metal-frame bunk beds lining the walls. No one inside was wearing a uniform. They all looked up at me, an American in prison fatigues, and I could see the surprise on their faces. What are *you* doing here?

I was escorted to cell 108 in wing #1 of the prison. I nodded to them and said hello in Arabic. They returned the greeting, and a couple welcomed me in English. My cellmates gave me a top bunk right in the middle of the room. The most coveted berths, it turned out, were bottom bunks closest to the walls at either end of the room.

Despite being given the rookie's bunk, and possibly being a foreign spy or terrorist in their eyes, I was given a touchingly warm welcome. They saw I had absolutely nothing with me, not even a toothbrush. They, by contrast, had bags of stuff stashed under their bunks. Inmates here were allowed visitors, so their relatives could bring them food, clothes, or even money to buy things in the commissary. I even once saw someone come around selling ice cream. They immediately offered me their help. I was given some shorts and a T-shirt, and one of my new cellmates even gave me his toothbrush. There is probably nothing more generous in this world than spontaneously lending a toothbrush to a total stranger. There's not much that is less hygienic either, but I was desperate to brush my teeth after more than a month without being able to, so I gratefully accepted.

This all seemed like a vast improvement from Branch 215. I quickly learned that Adra is a large, general-purpose prison on the northeastern edge of Damascus. With a population of approximately ten thousand, it is like a small town rather than a prison, with a whole variety of prisoners inside. A portion of the men at Adra, many of whom spoke English and quickly became my good friends, were in prison on "terrorism" charges. That is, they had taken part in peaceful protests against the regime and been tortured and jailed for years, some of them for life. One had simply been returning from a high school trip to neighboring Jordan when the authorities grabbed and accused him. They were former students, air-conditioner salesmen, drywall installers, and chicken farmers. In the cell next door was even a man who had once been the CEO of a large Syrian technology company, along with four of his colleagues, each of whom was exceptionally kind and hospitable to me. These were all seemingly ordinary people who had been swept up in extraordinarily brutal times.

This is not to say there weren't actual criminals, possibly even terrorists, at Adra too. One day while I was jogging in the prison yard, an inmate approached me. I could tell from his body language that he was trying to initiate a conversation with me, but his demeanor seemed to indicate that he wanted to do so discreetly.

He quietly pulled me aside. "Sam, I was in ISIS," he said. That was a little alarming for an American to hear up close. But he didn't mean any harm. "I was in prison in Russia for two years and now I've been in prison in Syria for two more. You're going to get out of here, and when you do, please go to the CIA and tell them I'm here. I don't want to be in prison in Syria or Russia. I'd rather be in Guantánamo, it is much nicer."

To this day, that man remains among the sketchiest humans I've ever met. He was always nice to me, but I was a bit cautious about interacting with him.

Almost every morning at Adra I would change into the shorts and T-shirt that had been loaned to me by my new cellmates and head outside to the all-concrete prison yard. It was swelteringly hot, but I ran till I tired myself out. My fellow inmates watched and were naturally curious about my exercise routine. It felt wonderful to be outside, despite the unforgiving Damascus summer sun, and to be able to actually talk to people.

In the evenings, my fellow inmates would often invite me to join them for food. They were excellent cooks despite the limited ingredients we had to work with. They also occasionally had access to a sweet Middle Eastern dessert called halawa, which I came to love and ate directly from the tub the few times it was available. I always thanked my new friends for their generous welcome. It was bewildering to experience warm hospitality in a Syrian prison, a place I perhaps would have expected to only encounter ill-intentioned people. About a week into my time at Adra, I approached my new friend Elliot, an older man, about this observation.

"Sam," he said, "in Syria, all the good people are here in prison, because all the bad people are outside putting us in here."

TAG GOODWIN

The news from Joseph that Sam was alive in Syria was like a sugar rush. It lifted us up for several days. But with limited information to follow it up, except for assurances from the man in Connecticut, we started to experience a crash again. By the last weekend in June, it felt like we were running out of steam.

Ann was feeling it too. She admitted that this was the first time since Sam vanished over a month earlier that it seemed like not much was happening. Despite establishing scores of leads, we still had what seemed to be virtually zero concrete information. The weight of all those stern warnings—of the FBI constantly telling us to manage expectations, of Ambassador Ford informing us we would probably never see our son again—was discouraging and was starting to make us wonder if all of our efforts were for naught.

We still moved forward as vigorously as we could, of course. I was chasing down new leads every day, and Ann's group of prayer warriors, still unaware of the intention, was still active around the clock. My extended family members, who were now aware of the case but sworn to secrecy, had lit candles in their homes all across America and sent us pictures to boost our spirits. Betty had also been sending us shots of prayer candles she had lit across Portugal and Spain as she walked the Camino. Despite these gestures, it was getting harder each day to remain hopeful.

I had spoken to George, the father of Stephanie Hajjar, several times about his brother-in-law Joseph. Aside from reassurances that he was working on the case, there was nothing new. I managed to persuade George to let me speak directly to Joseph in Connecticut. He agreed, but Joseph himself was no more forthcoming. Joseph did sound confident in the ability of his "friend" and even said to me that "we are family and my friend will not let us down," which was encouraging, but it was also frustrating to be so utterly in the dark on an issue of such vital importance to us all.

In late June, Joseph asked something extraordinary of me. He said that all of our other efforts to contact Assad were interfering with his friend's work and asked us to stop them all.

At Joseph's request, I had not told anyone—neither the Team SG23 network nor the Fusion Cell—who he was, not even Ann or Luke. When I finally told the SG23 group that we were now being asked to shut down all of our channels, they asked, not unreasonably, "Are we really going to stop everything we're doing because some guy named 'Joe from Connecticut' says so?"

Could I take such a leap of faith with someone I didn't even know?

I spent that last weekend of June—which was now day 37 of Sam's disappearance—talking it through with various people I trusted.

That Sunday morning, things unexpectedly and dramatically became even more convoluted. Ann and I were at home, talking to Ben Stephan on Ann's phone, when an unknown number flashed up on my cell.

It was a 305 area code, which I knew was Miami.

"Probably just spam," I said. "I'm not answering that."

"TAG!" Ann shouted. "You've got to answer every call that comes our way now!"

"Okay, okay," I muttered. I walked into the bedroom to take the call.

A man with a very thick Middle Eastern accent started speaking in broken English.

"Hello," he said. "Is this Thomas Goodwin, father of Samwell Goodwin?"

I was almost too surprised to answer. "Yes, yes," I said. "Who am I talking to?"

The man didn't offer a name or anything by way of an explanation. "I have a note from your son. From Samwell."

I rushed out of the bedroom and motioned to Ann, who was still speaking with Ben, to come listen. I put my own cell on speaker so Ann and Ben could both hear.

"You have a note from Sam?" I asked.

"Yes," said the man, "a message from Samwell, I will read to you."

Ann stared at me, both of us stunned. With great presence of mind, though, she grabbed a piece of paper and a pen. The mystery man began reading a note he said was from our son.

Thomas Goodwin, it began, followed by my phone number.

> *Safe—alive*
> *Adraa Prison—Damascus Central Prison*
> *USA Embassy in Beirut—I need legal/consular help!*
> *I always order the salmon when eating at the Missouri*
> *Athletic Club.*

As the man read the message, Ann scrambled to keep up. With his heavy accent and the sheer surprise, she kept asking him to repeat himself. Ben was also taking notes on his end. I asked the man if he could send us a screenshot of the note. He said he would. While attempting to obtain as much information as possible, but not do anything that might spook the man and cause him to end the call, Ann asked him if he could get a message back to Sam.

"I think so," he said.

"Please tell Sam we love him and we're working on bringing him home," Ann replied desperately.

We then asked again if he could send us a picture of the note.

He reiterated that he would but then hung up, having delivered his startling message.

Ann and I stood anxiously, wondering what exactly had just happened and if the man would actually make good on his promise to send a photo. Less than a minute later, there was a ping as it landed on my phone. We opened it and stared at the note. It certainly looked like Sam's writing. Ann took my phone and forwarded it to herself. But in the turmoil of the moment, she accidentally forwarded it to a different Anne, a friend of the family. Within a minute, this other Anne called me in a panic, wondering what on earth was going on. She sounded almost hysterical and Ann had to assume her school administrator's voice to order her not to breathe a word to anyone because lives might depend on it. Cowed but somewhat calmed, Anne just kept on saying, "Yes, ma'am, no, ma'am," and readily agreed as we hung up. We later learned that Anne and her family had just bought a new puppy. In honor of Sam and in hopes of him coming home safely, they named their puppy Sammy and continued to support our efforts with prayer.

We all quickly got back to the note. Though we were one hundred percent sure it was Sam's handwriting and that only Sam would know that he always ordered the salmon when we went out for a meal at the Missouri Athletic Club, there was no date on the note and no way of knowing if he had written it, perhaps, with a gun to his head, or even if he was still alive today, for that matter. We tried calling the man back, but it seemed as if he had used a burner phone for the call and then ditched it. In any case, this was a sign that Sam had been alive at some point since his disappearance, and he appeared to be in a Syrian prison.

David Bradley and Luke Hartig had already briefed us on the prison system. From what we recalled, Adra was believed to be the least bad of all of them, although still not a place anyone would want to spend time. If Sam was there, it was at the very least a positive sign. But was any of this true? Had someone coerced him to write the note as a way of throwing us off the scent of where he really might be? There was no way of knowing. Ann called the Fusion Cell to see what they made of it. They were baffled that Sam would be able to facilitate any communication out of Syria. They told us to forward the note to them along with some samples of Sam's penmanship for the forensic handwriting expert to compare. Ann went down to Sam's room in the basement where he kept some of his old French homework from high school. She scanned a few pages and sent them to the FBI. Within twenty-four hours, they had confirmed the handwriting was Sam's.

We had our first real lead.

SAM GOODWIN

Adra was a vast upgrade from Branch 215. I was able to move around, exercise outside, and, perhaps most important, speak with other humans.

Unfortunately, though, in talking to the men around me, many of whom would become close friends, I discovered the sheer brutality of the regime that now controlled my fate.

One of them was a guy my age named Albert, whose father ran a chimney-building company outside Damascus. He was a university student who spoke pretty good English. I tended to naturally gravitate toward the English speakers, and we quickly became friends. Albert told me much later that when I first entered the cell, all the prisoners had assumed I was an American spy, or possibly a jihadist or a terrorist. Despite that, they gave me a warm welcome. At the very least, the idea of me possibly being a CIA agent gave me some curiosity value. There were, as I had discovered, already a couple of self-proclaimed ISIS members in the room.

Albert had been arrested after a protest against the regime five years earlier and was thrown in Sednaya Prison, which I learned was even worse than Branch 215. By comparison, Adra felt like a badly run summer camp. Albert and many of the others had been through the horrors of Sednaya. As they told me their grim stories, they would pull up a sleeve of their T-shirt or the leg of their pants to show me huge livid scars where they had been beaten, whipped, burned, and shocked. One of the men told me his interrogators had held a blowtorch to his genitals and ordered him to confess. He had confessed, of course, and was now serving a long prison sentence for "terrorism."

Others recounted the horrors of the special "security" prisons, like Branch 215, where I had spent a month. These were men who had been through hell and yet they soldiered on, all hoping that one day they would get back to their families or somehow escape from Syria. I listened to their stories and saw their battered bodies, and I selfishly worried that I too might have to face the same someday soon.

My new friends assured me that Adra was the least dangerous of Assad's prisons, with family visits and shops and services. In addition to people selling food and cigarettes, there were ingenious repairmen who could fix broken electric razors or make a basketball pump out of a water bottle. There were even some tattered English paperback books, which I figured would be great for preserving my sanity. If only I could get my hands on some prescription glasses, as my vision is poor and my contact lenses had expired weeks earlier.

There were people from so many walks of life in Adra that you could find all sorts of things that the prison itself didn't provide, including an optometrist. I quickly paid a visit to this doctor—himself an inmate—who had managed to procure a clunking piece of equipment for eye tests that looked like an antique from the 1940s. He did a few tests on his rickety machine and then wrote me a receipt. He said he would order my glasses as soon as I paid. The price wasn't much, just a few dollars, but the problem was that I simply didn't have any money at all.

When I returned to the cell, my roommates asked why I didn't have any glasses on. I rather sheepishly explained that I didn't have money to buy them. The next morning, three of my new friends came up to me and said, "Sam, we talked to the doctor and paid for your glasses. You should have them by the end of this week."

I was overwhelmed by their generosity. Having now been detained for more than six weeks, this was one of my brightest moments. These men who barely knew me, and who themselves had been so horribly abused, had banded together to help me, out of sheer human kindness. It reminded me of why I had set out on my travels in the first place—to meet and connect with good, ordinary people all around the world—and made me determined to return the favor in any way I could. Since I was the only American any of these men would ever meet, I swore to do my best to give them a good impression of myself and my country.

There were no cell phones allowed in Adra, but I was surprised to discover there was a public telephone attached to the wall of the dormitory. Almost around the clock, there was someone standing there, speaking to his relatives. Could it be that simple to get a message out? I asked my friends and my hopes were immediately crushed when they told me it could only be used for calls inside Syria and in Arabic.

But the phone did give me an idea as to how I could maybe communicate with the outside world.

STEPHANIE (STEPH) GOODWIN

That first weekend in July, my dad's brother Justin had invited our family up to his lakeside cabin in Sunapee, New Hampshire, for the weekend. Mom and Dad couldn't make it—they were in DC that weekend, having meetings about Sam. None of my other siblings could make it either, so I went alone and hung out for a long weekend, spending mornings on the lake and afternoons on the deck of the house. We had recently told Uncle Justin and his family about Sam, so they were being very supportive. It was nice to be out in the country, surrounded by people I could actually talk to about what we were going through.

It was Saturday afternoon, and we had spent the morning on the water. I was tired and just lying on the couch in the living room to chill when I felt my phone vibrate. I looked at it and there was a new message on Instagram from someone with a strange username.

"Hello, I'm Dinah, your brother is with my brother in the prison. Sam wants to know if TAG has been able to communicate with the US embassy. 'Tell Slan and B happy birthday.'"

I leaped up from the couch, excitement instantly obliterating my fatigue. I think I was dialing my dad's number before I'd even finished reading the message. Almost immediately, Mom was also on the call. We could barely contain our excitement, though Dad urged caution.

"Wow, this is crazy," he said. As he quickly noted, it could be real, but it might also be the Syrian regime trying to entrap us somehow.

"How are we going to respond?" I asked.

I sent my parents the Instagram message so they could scrutinize it too, while I scrolled through Dinah's feed, seeing what else she might have posted and who she was friends with. No actual posts and no followers. A few friends with Arabic names, following some celebrity and musical profiles. There was no clue about the real nature of the person who sent it. What kind of young person doesn't have any posts on Instagram? It could easily have been a bot. Or a setup.

Yet once again, there was a very personalized message. My mom quickly figured out the strange reference to "Slan" in the message. Sam's affectionate nickname for her was Flan—a riff on

Ann—and clearly through the game of geopolitical telephone it had become "Slan." It was indeed her birthday in a few days. And "B" was obviously Betty, as that is what Sam calls her, whose birthday was the very next day, July 7. The message had undoubtedly come from Sam.

My mom decided the only thing to do was to run it by the Fusion Cell—this was their field of expertise, after all. They suspected it could well be the regime, since they had not heard of any other hostages who had managed to smuggle communication out of a Syrian prison. Therefore the response needed to be strictly neutral, with nothing that might be interpreted as a coded message to Sam. They spent the rest of the day working on a suitable answer, while we all jumped on WhatsApp with the SG23 group to discuss the new development. Most of the team was inclined to believe Dinah was a fake.

"Something doesn't seem right about this Dinah. What young person has no posts?" said Father Vigoa.

"Agree. I think it's definitely a fake/newly created account," added my brother David.

But Rob, who had traveled with Sam in the Middle East, made an important observation. "I don't know. Remember that in the Arab world, girls posting photos of themselves is highly frowned upon, so the zero posts may not be as suspicious."

He also checked out the accounts of Dinah's alleged friends and found that they all seemed to be about the same age, and several followed one another. Most were Syrians, and the content they posted all appeared to be age-appropriate. Those were all the hallmarks of a real, organic account.

Maybe she was real after all. It was worth taking a chance, we eventually decided.

Mom was so excited by all this that she asked Betty to buy Sam a new outfit since we didn't know if he had clothes to wear home. Betty also made up a toiletry bag for Sam, with new contact lenses, glasses, and his laptop and charger. They packed up all the new gear in a bag and put it with Mom and Dad's "go bags"—a couple of small suitcases they had already packed so that they could leave at a moment's notice in the event Sam were to ever be released.

When the FBI got back to us six hours later, they advised us to keep the message very simple but encouraging. Something along the lines of, "Stay strong, keep the faith, we love you." Eight words after six hours—it wasn't much for first contact with a brother who had vanished into a foreign prison.

But I dutifully kept it simple. "Thank you so much Dinah. Is there anything else you can tell me about my brother? Are you able to get a message back to him?"

Dinah was quick to respond. "He's waiting for an answer from you. Sure. I'll tell my brother and he'll tell Sam."

This time, I was so excited by the contact that I didn't bother to run my follow-up message by the Fusion Cell experts and have to wait for hours.

"Thank you. Please tell Sam that I love him, to stay strong, and I can't wait to eat a Chipotle burrito together. When are you able to get this message to him? Thank you again!"

I added the personalized touch about Chipotle because we had always loved going there together to eat burritos and I wanted Sam to know for sure that the message had come from me. But when the Fusion Cell found out during a secure conference call what I had said, they were furious. They said that could easily be taken by the Syrians for a coded message, and that I had put my brother in severe danger as a result.

"You're only supposed to write back what we tell you. *Chipotle* could be a code word and they could kill him thinking he's a spy!" one of them said.

I was devastated, but Mom was also on the call and she stepped in to defend me, although they must have been pretty shocked too. But that's what parents do.

When Dinah wrote back later that day, we were all encouraged. "Tonight my brother will call me i will tell him that, Sam with him in the same room, so he will get the message directly. You're welcome."

And I prayed. "Please, please God, let this be real."

The next day, we received a new message. "Good evening. Sam said that he love you and can't wait to eat Chipotle burrito too. And asked if the Blues won the cup??"

The relief flooded through me. I hadn't gotten my brother killed or tortured. And if Sam was asking about whether his hockey team had won the Stanley Cup, he was clearly not in too bad of shape. Incredibly, the St. Louis Blues had in fact won that year, for the first time in franchise history.

We sent this good news back to Sam, despite Rob joking that perhaps we shouldn't because Sam might never believe the Blues had finally won the Cup, since the team had a long history of choking in the playoffs. He might think *he* was the one being duped!

SAM GOODWIN

Elliot was a man in his fifties who had been jailed on charges of financial corruption, an accusation he said was fabricated. That was something I could easily believe, having seen the Syrian justice system up close myself. Elliot had a trim gray beard and walked with a stoop, the result of having been savagely beaten across his back with a wooden paddle by the Sednaya guards. Of all the inmates in my wing, he probably spoke English the best, and we would spend long periods of time talking. After a couple of weeks, when the prisoners had gotten to know me a little and realized I was not, in fact, a spy, Elliot approached me and told me he had devised a way for me to get a message out to my family.

"Tomorrow is laundry day," he said. "My friend will bring me clean clothes and I will give him my dirty clothes to take away and wash. You can give me a note and I will put it in my pocket and my friend will take it out and pass it on to your family."

I was stunned that he would take such a risk on my behalf, but he insisted it was not too dangerous. The guards rarely searched dirty laundry. They were more concerned about items coming *into* the prison, not out. I had to write the note in a rush, since the guards were at that very moment about to start moving us back into our respective cells, and Elliot was in the one next to mine. I quickly wrote a note with my father's name and phone number, telling him I was alive and being held at Adra Prison. Elliot took the note and looked at it.

"Sam, I think you should add a clue to this note. So if it makes it to your father, he'll know for sure it came from you," he said.

That hadn't even occurred to me. I was, after all, new to this business of smuggling secret messages out of prison. I quickly scrawled a line: "I always order the salmon when eating at the Missouri Athletic Club." Then I gave it to Elliot as he was ordered back to his cell by the guards.

Then…nothing. Over the next week or so, I never heard if the note had been delivered, though Elliot informed me it had, at least, not been confiscated by the Adra guards. Realizing I might never know if it made it to my family, I decided to try a second path of communication.

Albert, the former university student, appeared to trust me by this point. I talked a great deal with him and another guy our age named Arthur, who had worked with his brother and cousin at a drywalling company before prison, and who also spoke proficient English. It's eye-opening how long and fruitful conversations can be when there are no phones as distractions, no meetings to attend, no television shows to watch, and no kids to take care of. I'd tell them about America, not the politics or history, but the everyday stuff they were interested in, about how Tinder worked and the best places to eat or travel, or the wonders of social media, which they'd hardly had time to experience since it was taking off just as they were being dragged off to a life in jail.

Some of these conversations could be a comedy of manners. One day, Albert asked me, "Sam, how does Adra compare to prison in America?"

I laughed. "I don't know, Albert, I've never been in prison in America!" He had just assumed, from his experience in Syria, that everyone goes to jail at some point, no matter where they live.

As we were now friends, I asked Albert if there was anyone he could call on the Adra phone who might be able to pass on a message to my family in the States. He thought about it and then said he could ask his sister the next time she called. Her name was Dinah, he explained, and she had an Instagram account she could use to reach out to my family.

This was great news. One problem, though. In the United States, we are so used to our phones remembering everything for us that it is quite hard to actually remember the precise social media handles of even our closest friends and family. As I thought which sibling Dinah should contact, I started with the oldest but found I couldn't quite remember the exact handles of my brothers, Paul and David. When I got to Steph, I was relieved that I was able to remember hers exactly. I told Albert to relay pretty much the same message I had given to Elliot but with a different personalized touch to show them it was me. "Happy birthday to Flan and B." My mom and my sister Betty would easily recognize my nicknames for them.

To my surprise, the next time Albert spoke to his sister, several days later, he had received a message back from Steph. An actual message from my sister! I had reached out from a Syrian prison and managed to connect with my family at home. I was elated, not least because I knew they would be. They now knew I was alive and able to communicate with them. This changed everything and filled me with renewed hope that I might just make it out of this nightmare.

Of course, Albert had to memorize Steph's response, which his sister had read out to him over the phone. We met during the period when the different cells were allowed to mingle in the communal outside area for a few hours each day. Not surprisingly, he got a bit confused when it came to the part where Steph mentioned how she was looking forward to sharing a Chipotle burrito together, never having heard of such a thing in his life.

"'Tell Sam I love him, to stay strong, and"—Albert then got a somewhat puzzled look on his face as he attempted to concentrate—"Steph says she wants to eat with you a 'chippolay toledo'?"

When I realized what he was trying to say, I actually jumped up and down in the courtyard. "It's a Chipotle burrito!" At that moment, I knew this was a real message from Steph and that we now had a secret channel from Adra Prison in Syria back to Nashville and St. Louis.

FATHER VIGOA

My outreach to the Syrian patriarch's office was seemingly beginning to pay off. Syria's Christian leaders have always needed to tread a fine diplomatic line with the country's political leaders. Various patriarchs have been labeled as being pro-regime, as many Christians do not like the authoritarian leadership. But it's been a tough and delicate balancing act for them to carry out, keeping their communities as safe as possible while not endorsing the horrors carried out by the government that purports to shield them.

For our purposes, this meant the Patriarchy of the Syriac Orthodox Church had a line to the president, and that was exactly what the FBI had told us we needed to save Sam.

Now it looked like that was bearing some fruit. I received an email from the patriarch's office. Part of his email read:

Dear Fr. Richard,

We did our best to explain to the office of the President the case of Sam Goodwin.

We were told that the investigation had to fairly proceed and he will be released, as soon as no suspicious incrimination would take place. This is the normal procedure followed by every country and Syrian government is well open to treat with justice people. I am confident he will be released.

We pray for the needed peace in Syria as well for justice on behalf of innocent people suffering because of the unjust sanctions against this country.

Patriarch Ignatius Youssef III

The mention of "unjust sanctions" made me wonder who else might have seen the communication. No doubt the regime expected such platitudes from church leaders and had its eyes on any communications with the outside world. Nevertheless, it was encouraging that we were apparently closing in on Assad's inner circle.

SAM GOODWIN

There were a handful of interesting and somewhat surprising characters at Adra. After a few weeks, I was told by my new friends in wing #1 that in wing #4 was a guy named Adam whose family had spent time living in the United States. His father was a doctor and his mother was a dentist. They had worked in Boston and Pennsylvania in the 1980s and '90s. Adam had been born there and still had three siblings living in Bloomington, Indiana. Given this background, I believed he might be able to help me.

The challenge, however, was that we were not allowed to mix with inmates in other wings. The only time I was ever taken out of wing #1 was to go to court. Prison life, however, makes people resourceful, and my friends devised a scheme to get me in front of Adam.

It turned out that Adam had followed in his mother's footsteps and trained as a dentist. Now, at Adra, he had been sent to work in the prison's health center. My friends got creative and told me to fake being sick. I'd had plenty of practice with this from Branch 215 and, for obvious reasons, was a little wary of doing it again. But my cellmates reassured me it wouldn't take much. Sure enough, the guards allowed for me to be escorted to the sick bay. Adam's English wasn't great, and he didn't seem overly keen on helping, but he said he would see what he could do.

I returned to wing #1 and only saw Adam one more time, so I had no idea if anything would come of the plan. But at least I now had three potential channels open to the United States.

TAG GOODWIN

It was a Sunday morning, around half past nine. I was at home when a WhatsApp message pinged on my phone. I opened it and was confused to see what appeared to be an advertisement in Arabic for dental surgery. The country code on the phone number was 963, which I knew by this point was Syria.

I tapped on the image to get a better look. A dark-haired woman in a white lab coat was holding up one of those tiny mirrors dental surgeons use to inspect teeth. As I was scratching my head, another message appeared underneath the first. This time it was a text, in English.

"Hello, I'm trying to reach Mr. Thomas," it said.

"Yes," I typed. "How can I help?"

"Am I speaking to him? How is your family?"

I was thinking about what to say to that when the next message appeared. "Are you missing any?"

"How is your son?"

"What was his name? He sent you hello."

"But I need to be sure I am speaking to his father…!"

Whoever it was had my full attention by now. I typed in as fast as I could, "Yes, this is Thomas, Sam's father. Who is this? What information do you have about my son?"

The name of this interlocutor was Hellen. "I'm a dentist. My son is in Syrian gail since 4 years. He is Syrian-American. He met your son in gail and spoke with him. Your son asked my son to help him contact with his father. Because no one knows where he is."

She added: "I contacted the Czech embassy who are helping to free my son. I told him about your son and asked them to help him. And I gave them your number." Of course, we had been told the Czech embassy in Damascus was handling US matters in Syria in the absence of any formal diplomatic ties, but we had never contacted them directly ourselves, on the advice of the Fusion Cell.

"I hope you and your son the best. And I hope I helped."

I was just typing a response when she added, a little self-consciously, "Gail = prison."

I didn't immediately respond in any more depth. There were too many things going through my head. It seemed like a huge breakthrough to potentially have someone who could have almost direct contact with Sam. But who was she? Was she really a person, or was this some regime trick to lure us into a trap of some sort? Just like the mystery caller with the note from Sam, there seemed to be no way of verifying her identity. So I had Ann contact the Fusion Cell and relay all the messages to them, asking how they suggest we proceed.

With their resources, they confirmed within a day or so that the woman really was a dentist in Damascus whose Syrian American son was in Adra Prison. We then discussed what I should write back, something simple and heartfelt that would give Sam hope but not put him—or the dentist and her son—in any kind of danger. This all took time, so it was a couple of days before I responded. That was difficult, wanting desperately to reach out and send a message back to Sam, but having to wait for it all to be cleared.

"Hi Hellen, yes you were very helpful. We have not heard anything through the official channels so your message brought much comfort to our family. Thank you for all you did with the Czech embassy. I cannot imagine being without my son for four years and what you are going through. You and your son helped bring our family peace of mind that Sam is doing well and connected with kind people. It would comfort our family if you could occasionally ask how Sam is doing. Thank you and your son again for helping connect us with Sam."

It was a few hours before she responded. When she did, she said she visited her son at Adra every other Monday and could pass on messages to Sam. She also said that when she went, she usually passed some money to her son—20,000 Syrian pounds, which she said was around $40, as well as some clothes. She said she would ask if Sam needed anything.

Now, this was all great news, although we were naturally a little suspicious about the money. We had been warned we would be targets for a shakedown. But the amount was trifling, and besides, we had no idea how to transfer money to Syria, which has so many sanctions slapped on it that it is almost unreachable by the international banking system. So the question seemed moot for now.

PART VI

FREEDOM'S CHESSBOARD

ANN GOODWIN

P rayer had gotten me through the agonizing first days of Sam's captivity, when it seemed there was no hope. Now that there was a glimmer of hope, it seemed more important than ever to pray.

Then, on July 13, Steph received a new Instagram message from Dinah.

"I want to tell you that Sam has a civil court on July 16 and wants to know if you will send anyone or if there's anyone in the court by you…"

I was immediately on the phone with the Fusion Cell. By this point, a strange dynamic had emerged between the agents in the group and me. After TAG had decided to no longer speak with them because they were slowing him down, I became the family's point person in liaising with their team. This likely flagged to them that we were not too satisfied with their performance. But it did result in me having a certain kind of leverage.

One conversation I had with them clearly startled the woman who organized the group meetings. I told her I wanted to have an update meeting with the Fusion Cell, but that there were only four people I wanted in the meeting. I was handpicking these people based on who, over the past six weeks, I had determined to be the most helpful. The woman said my request could be arranged but asked if a particular senior member of the Fusion Cell could also join, as this was their standard process and structure. By this point, after a month and a half of engagements, I knew who this person was, and he was not someone I needed at this time. Not only was he not needed, but he consistently talked too much and even slowed us down.

"Okay, fine," I replied. "He can come to the meeting too, as long as he doesn't speak." There was a long pause on the phone. Clearly, this woman had never before experienced a family making these types of demands of the FBI. It turned out, though, we had that meeting, and the senior official sat in it quietly.

Hellen later texted with additional information and was becoming increasingly specific. Sam's arraignment was to be held at ten o'clock local time. "He needs somebody with him," she added. We felt helpless. Since we couldn't actually be there for Sam, I figured the next best thing was to be in church praying for him at the exact moment he was in court.

TAG wrote back to Hellen, saying, "Please let Sam know that we are working on getting him assistance and that we send our love." It was hard sending such boilerplate messages, but the FBI warned us that it was more than likely that the regime could see these communications. We couldn't risk the safety of our intermediaries.

Ten in the morning in Damascus is two in the morning in St. Louis, but that wasn't going to deter us. I set my alarm to head out for the Eucharistic adoration chapel at St. Clement of Rome Catholic

Church, our home parish, at a quarter to two. I was so touched when Betty, Steph, and Steph's fiancé, Matt, joined me. I was even more moved when my friend Kathy—whom I had told about Sam at the outset, so she could buy me some clothes for his funeral—also showed up, with her husband, as did my sister Christi and our family friend Katie. The Holy Spirit was clearly present. Together we prayed intensely as the moment approached when we thought Sam would be appearing before the judge thousands of miles away.

As we bowed in devotion, both Betty and I held our phones, waiting for Sam to call saying the judge had dismissed his case. We waited. And waited. An hour passed. The call never came.

Going home in the middle of the night with no news was a painful reminder that even though we were making progress, Sam was still in a prison cell on the other side of the world. Throughout that day, we heard nothing. TAG called Joe from Connecticut. He too had heard nothing but assured us that the judge and the court appearance was all mere window dressing and a regime sideshow. It was *his* contact who would get Sam out. Since we had no idea what any of that involved, it was not very reassuring.

It was two agonizing days before we learned more. Joseph called to say that the court appearance had been delayed but stressed that it made no difference anyway. Then Hellen sent a message confirming the delay, but with a twist that was like a gut punch. "Sam needs support and help!" she said. "My son just called and told me. My son and friend in prison are taking care of him. Your son is not in the same room now."

Was Sam cracking? Freaking out after his court date was postponed? He'd been in prison for almost two months now; was his hope running out? I didn't think so. I kept reminding myself how strong and resourceful my son is, but our family was starting to worry that things were taking a turn for the worse.

A few days later, we got another message from Dinah. "Sam wants you to know that on July 16 there wasn't any decision yet and the judge waits for a reply to the letter they sent to the US embassy in Damascus. Sam says please follow up the process."

Again, this was Kafkaesque. The Syrian judge was writing letters to an embassy that had been closed for seven years and waiting for a reply that might never come? While our son was sitting in a jail cell, possibly losing all hope, we're waiting for a reply from the embassy in Damascus? The Fusion Cell said it was not possible for the embassy to reply since there were no diplomatic ties. What on earth were we supposed to do?

We brainstormed ways to get a more substantive message to Sam and to let him know we were using all possible means to get him out, without potentially landing either Hellen or Dinah in trouble with the regime too. We couldn't tell him about Joseph or any of the dozen other back channels we were pursuing because that might compromise the work they were doing. Then Dinah wrote back. "There will be another court appearance on July 31."

That was another fifteen days away! I wasn't sure how we could endure another two weeks. But one thing was sure—for Sam it was going to be even harder.

TAG called Joseph to see if he had any updates. I still had no idea who the guy was, and I was deeply skeptical. As usual, he told TAG that his friend would get Sam out, but that he had been exceptionally busy for the past two weeks. Obviously, for us, we couldn't imagine what could be so important that it would keep someone from doing everything they could to free our son.

"For me, my patience is waning," TAG told him.

After the call, TAG was frustrated, not because he didn't trust or believe in Joseph, but because everything was moving slowly. As a result, TAG got on a conference call with Team SG23. Several of the task force members were beginning to lose confidence in the Lebanese path, but TAG reiterated to the group his confidence in Joseph. He then also wisely pressed on by asking everyone to bring forth all other ideas they had, in the event that Joseph's friend did in fact fail to bring Sam home.

There were countless balls in the air at this point, as we were in touch with so many people. Sam had a friend from Singapore who had a connection to CNN's Christiane Amanpour. We were considering approaching Democratic presidential hopeful Tulsi Gabbard, who had controversially gone to Damascus to meet Assad, though we worried she would not be very discreet and potentially use it as leverage for her campaign. We were talking to NGOs and security experts working in the region. We'd had meetings with our state's senators, while Father Vigoa had gotten in touch with Senator Marco Rubio in Florida and Miami mayor Francis Suarez, both of whom he knew personally.

On July 22, we noticed something interesting in the news. Several outlets, including *Vatican News*, the Catholic News Agency, and the Italian publication known by its abbreviation *SIR*, covered a notable meeting that had taken place earlier that day in Damascus. The Vatican press office reported that Cardinal Peter Turkson, prefect of the

Dicastery for Promoting Integral Human Development, and Cardinal Mario Zenari, apostolic nuncio to Syria, met that morning with Assad at the presidential palace. During the meeting, Turkson and Zenari delivered a letter from Pope Francis, in which the pope expressed to Assad his broad concern for the ongoing crisis in Syria. The letter outlined several specific issues, including the plight of refugees, continued war violence, and civilians' lack of access to humanitarian aid. According to news reports, the letter also made specific mention of an additional concern. It discussed the "plight and release of political prisoners" and said the family members of these people "must be given access to information about their loved ones." Cardinal Pietro Parolin, who was not in the meeting but serves as the Vatican's secretary of state, was quoted saying that political prisoners are "particularly close to the heart of Pope Francis."

We had no way of knowing for sure whether any of this was in regard to Sam. But we did know a few things for sure. In June, Father Vigoa communicated by phone and email with Cardinal Zenari about Sam. He said he would try to help, but in order to engage on the case, he needed to get permission from Rome. Now, in July, Cardinal Zenari met in person with Assad, delivering a message from Pope Francis. In the letter, there was specific mention of political prisoners in Syria and granting their families access to information about their status and well-being. Given these facts, we believed it was possible that Pope Francis had personally made efforts to free Sam from captivity.

Although this information via our Catholic Church contacts was encouraging, we continued to consider the Lebanese path to be plan A.

We were informed that the Lebanese government and the US embassy in Beirut had finally been in touch. It had apparently taken forever because they had to move through official diplomatic channels. The Lebanese had sought official confirmation that Sam was just a simple traveler and not a spy, so they could reassure the Syrians.

What was interesting for us was that we had not approached the Lebanese government ourselves. We wondered who had triggered this inquiry to the US embassy in Beirut.

SAM GOODWIN

Within a couple of weeks of my incarceration at Adra, I had gone from being a suspected spy to becoming a minor celebrity among the other inmates. Denied any other form of entertainment, having an American in their midst became an interesting novelty for many of them. I was constantly playing soccer, volleyball, and basketball with them in the exercise yard, or helping those studying English—their teacher himself an inmate—with their homework. I'd resolved to show them the best face of America by always being kind, respectful, and considerate, but at times it was exhausting work. There was zero privacy, and people were constantly coming to me, expecting me to be "on," like an A-list celebrity. Sam the traveler was always able to represent the United States well around the world, but it turns out Sam the prisoner was becoming fatigued and losing the energy to do so.

There was, however, at least one advantage to all this. I still didn't have any money for extra food, and the prison rations were pretty meager—rice, beans, and the occasional chunk of cucumber. Without me ever asking, my new students started giving me small amounts of money to help them out. It was more like a tip than payment, but it all added up for a man wearing donated eyeglasses and using a borrowed toothbrush. If they didn't have any cash to spare, they'd give me some food. One guy would often come to my bunk while I was reading, plop down a plate of chicken and rice, and pull out his English homework assignment. Even those who couldn't spare any food found a way to barter, giving me Arabic lessons in return. Within a few weeks, I was starting to put together basic sentences. I figured I could potentially be here for years, so it would certainly pay off to get started now. Elliot gave me a table of the Arabic alphabet and explained how to pronounce the characters. I practiced whenever I had a quiet moment. In an unexpected way, I had started my own business within the prison and was happy to work those entrepreneurial muscles.

It was an immense relief to have found a community, and I made some very good friends in Adra. But in the back of my mind, I was tormented by two things. I had no idea when—or even if—I would ever get out. And the stories the men had told me—every last one of them—of beatings and horrific torture gnawed away at me, making me wonder when it would be my turn.

On top of this, one day I was watching the local news on a neglected TV in our cell. This TV only worked sometimes. At night, my fellow inmates would often gather around to watch Turkish soap operas, but during the day they would watch any number of things. I obviously couldn't understand what the Syrian news reporter was saying because she was speaking in Arabic, but the supporting visuals were of bombs exploding. One of my cellmates translated for me. "Today, US-backed Israeli forces are bombing Damascus," he said. My facial reaction evolved from confusion to fear as my brain processed his words and the fact that I was genuinely in prison "behind enemy lines." Despite what I believed to be the potentially significant nature of this information, I was so overwhelmed with everything going on that I essentially just rolled my eyes and mentally added it to the growing list of issues I could do nothing about.

It was around this time that I made an important discovery. *Being* in prison was a lot less terrible than *thinking about* being in prison. If I could just focus on the power of the now, and not torture myself with all the what-ifs of my very uncertain future, then my quality of life improved vastly. I would try to focus exclusively on the present, on the right now. I'm lying on this bed, I'm reading a book, I'm eating food, and then I'm going to go run laps and I'll eat dinner and then go to sleep on this bed. This mindset made life infinitely better. I wasn't in any physical pain and had found friends and community. I could do this time, if I had to. When I got in trouble was when I let my imagination roam into the unknowable corridors of the future. I'm in jail in Syria, I could be in here forever, or I could be taken out tonight and tortured or even killed. This didn't do me any good. Unlike being in solitary, where the *now* had to be crushed by prayers, exercise, and telling stories to my imaginary friends and family, in Adra there was enough good for me to embrace and start living again. I guess we all do it in life—dwell on things that make us upset and less able to cope. In Adra, I learned the importance and power of focusing on being present in the moment.

A couple of days after being transferred to Adra, I was told to put on my black-and-white prison uniform. I was being taken to court. This was a cause for both hope and fear. I figured the judicial process in Syria was a sham, but part of me couldn't help but believe that if my case could just be processed, I would be closer to being released. After all, I knew it had all been one big mistake.

I was taken, along with several other inmates, back to the courthouse and police station where I had first been interviewed by a female judge when I was en route to Adra. Sure enough, the same woman was presiding over my case. Not surprisingly, I was offered neither a lawyer nor a translator, and the judge spoke very halting English. She explained that in my case, she was focusing on my purpose for coming to Syria. We would reconvene in the same courthouse in a couple of weeks.

To me, that didn't sound too awful, but then she went on in her stumbling English.

Once the facts of the case were established as to my purpose for coming to Syria, the judge said, I would serve whatever sentence needed to be served in Adra. Then, I would be transferred to a "security prison" until the authorities could determine if I was a spy or working with terrorists.

My heart sank. *Security prison.* Was that the black hole of Branch

215, of solitary confinement and torture cells? I wasn't sure I could bear to go back there after the relative calm of Adra. Gutted, I was led back to the meat van in chains with a deep sense of despair gnawing at my heart.

Back in cell 108, the others assured me the judge was wrong. "Adra is the last step before being released," Arthur told me. "You don't go from Adra *back* to security." That's the wrong direction.

Each of my inmate friends had different skills and connections, and collectively they did all they could to help me. It became challenging, however, to navigate this diverse mishmash of men. One of them, for example, seemed to consistently offer the most insightful information about Syria's network of prisons. Another knew the most about the country's judicial system. Another spoke the best English. Another I trusted the most. Another had actually traveled around the world a little bit and was relatively globally minded. Another I found to generally be the most empathetic.

It was encouraging to discover these attributes among my fellow inmates, but at the same time, it was troublesome because they were spread out among multiple people. I felt that in order for someone to concretely help me and provide genuine insight into my situation and what might happen, they needed to possess all of these qualities, and that just did not exist.

So who was I supposed to believe? The prisoners, informed by experience but also living in a world where the rules were arbitrarily made up by others? Or the judge, who appeared to speak for the regime that was holding me in this place? It was achingly frustrating.

ANN GOODWIN

It was barely seven in the morning on Wednesday, July 24—with still a week to go before Sam's next scheduled court appearance—when TAG got a phone call from Joseph. TAG was expecting the usual "no new developments, but my friend is on it" from the man in Connecticut, who had become a byword in our family for playing his cards close to his chest.

Not today. This time it was different.

Joseph said his friend had called him. Sam's release from Syria had been granted!

We were elated, but by now we had learned not to get *too* excited. It only made the endless disappointments that much harder to bear. Joseph had never before said anything as definitive as this. He told us to get ready, but there was no date set for the release. He believed his friend would go get Sam at some point in the next two weeks. But when? There were no more details, and he still refused to say who his contact was. I still didn't even know who *Joseph* was.

Of course, we immediately reported this to Team SG23, and I called the family. "Keep the prayers coming, thank you!"

There was no way Betty and I were going to miss midday Mass that day. We went to nearby St. Mary Magdalen Church in Brentwood, Missouri. When we got there, however, things started to get surreal.

During the homily, the priest began by announcing that today was the Feast of Saint Charbel. Neither of us had ever heard of this particular saint, but our ears pricked up when the priest explained that Charbel had been a monk in Lebanon in the nineteenth century and was revered for performing many miracles in his lifetime, as well as for his success in bringing Christians and Muslims together. His real name had been Yousef Makhlouf.

Yousef, the priest explained, is the Arabic version of the name *Joseph*.

"So if anyone here ever needs a miracle in Lebanon," the priest joked, "pray to Saint Charbel."

Betty and I looked at each other. Joseph from Connecticut, and a Lebanese miracle monk called Joseph? This had to be more than mere coincidence. This had to be divine intervention. Our hearts filled with hope, and we prayed to Saint Charbel with extra fervor for Sam to come home safely.

"May God's peace abundantly be with Sam and bring him home to us soon so he can live his life glorifying God," I wrote to the team in the SG23 WhatsApp chat.

When we got home, we told TAG all about this incredible moment. TAG decided to write to Joseph and his brother George—both of them Maronite Catholics—to let them know. He also sent them an old picture he had on his phone of our daughter Steph with George's daughter Stephanie, with a note of thanks for all they had done.

George wrote back, saying that when he told his wife the news that morning, she had cried with joy and started praying for us.

Joseph said he knew all about Saint Charbel and his propensity for miracles. In fact, it seems his shrine in the mountains above Beirut is famous in Lebanon—the Middle East's equivalent to Lourdes in France.

"I already pledged Sam to him," Joseph said. "We will visit his shrine when we get to Lebanon. In the meantime, be patient for just a little longer."

TAG GOODWIN

We didn't tell the Fusion Cell or our FBI case manager about Joseph's news. I didn't want anything to potentially snarl what now looked like our most promising lead.

The next day was a Thursday. I went in early to my office so I could complete as much work as possible should we need to move. It wasn't even nine in the morning when my phone rang. It was Joseph.

"My friend is picking up Sam tomorrow. You need to get to Beirut as fast as you possibly can. You will need to fly in with me, so we will need to meet in Europe and make a connection there. Paris would be best."

That was it. *Go time.* The moment we had all been waiting for.

I immediately called Ann. No answer. I called again, and then once more. Our son David was staying with us that week, so I called him. He had just woken up.

"Where's your mother?" I demanded. "She's not answering the phone."

"Sounds like she's in the shower," David said, sounding still half-asleep.

"Tell her to get ready now. We are going to Beirut. I need you to get on the computer and find us the first available flight via Europe."

"Got it. Shouldn't be hard," David said.

"Well, here's the catch. Joseph from Connecticut is coming too, and we have to enter Lebanon *with* him. Book him a flight too so we can meet up with him at an airport in Europe."

That made David's task more challenging, since Joseph was in Hartford, which does not have a well-connected international airport. Fortunately, due to all his travels around Europe for his hockey career, David, like Sam, is a master when it comes to online flight bookings. He found a flight for us at 11:55 a.m. that day, which was in only about ninety minutes, from St. Louis to Atlanta, with a very short connection that would get us to Paris the next morning to meet Joseph. Joseph would have to drive to Boston and catch a flight from there.

Steph had gone with Matt to Hoboken, New Jersey, to visit Paul and his girlfriend, Bridgid. Betty was at the St. Louis zoo that day with a family friend, together with her kids, to help pass the time as we sat on tenterhooks. As the news was breaking, Betty rushed home so she could help out with all the last-minute details. I put her and David in charge of fielding any communication from the government and media.

Ann and I already had our bags packed, along with items for Sam. We had no idea what the actual process might look like if Sam were to be freed. Could we book return flights for the next day? What sort of physical and mental state would he be in? Would he need to see a doctor or a therapist? Would he be allowed to fly out of Lebanon by the Lebanese authorities if he didn't have an entry stamp on his passport? We had no idea how he might be getting out of Syria—if indeed he really was—and there were a huge number of variables. Was any of this even going to happen? In the end, and even though it was much more expensive, we decided to buy one-way tickets and get the returns once we were there.

David drove Ann and me to the airport. To this day, I don't know how the FBI got wind of our departure, but they kept calling me incessantly. I let their calls go straight to voicemail. Eventually, they decided to call David, who was at the wheel. He picked up.

"David! Are your parents headed to Beirut?"

David looked at me in the passenger seat.

"Dad, are you going to Beirut?" he said.

"Yes," I answered. I wasn't going to tell them any more, and I had instructed all the kids not to either. Joseph was insistent that he and his mystery contact be kept strictly secret.

The FBI agent said they had urgent business. They wanted us to sign documents permitting them to track our phones while we were in Beirut. "If your parents don't sign these and anything happens to them in Beirut, David, we won't be able to track them. It's for their own safety."

I overheard this comment. "Fine," I conceded, grabbing the phone from David. "Meet us at the airport, then. But we're on a tight schedule, so we're not waiting for you if you're late."

Fifteen minutes later, we pulled up at Lambert, St. Louis's international airport. We were getting our bags out of the trunk when two black SUVs came tearing up to the drop-off area and stopped right behind us. The FBI agents jumped out holding documents. I signed them on the hood of their car and then Ann and I hurried inside to catch our flight to Atlanta.

The whole way, I was glancing at my watch, deeply nervous about any delay. I tried to reassure myself that if Sam was indeed getting out of Syria then he'd be safe even if we missed our flight. But after two months of extreme tension, I couldn't turn it off anymore. We just had to make it.

We made our connecting flight to Paris. We managed to get some sleep on the flight over the Atlantic, then woke up bleary-eyed but still nervous. We walked through the Charles de Gaulle airport, which was still reasonably quiet that early in the morning.

When we arrived at the departing gate for the flight to Beirut, standing there was "Joe from Connecticut."

JOSEPH ABBAS, *Lebanese American businessman*

In the early 1980s, I was an officer cadet in the Lebanese Military Academy, during one of the most turbulent periods of Lebanon's history. My country was in the middle of a bitter and protracted civil war. The main task of the armed forces was to try to protect the institutions of the state from attack or takeover by the various warring factions, which were mostly split along religious lines. The year I graduated, 1982, was the same year Israel invaded southern Lebanon to push back Palestinian guerrillas firing rockets across their northern border. The Israelis would stay for almost two decades, sparking the creation of Hezbollah, a Shia military group that has become a powerful political force in the country.

At the academy, I shared a dorm with a bunch of other guys. One of them was a cadet named Abbas Ibrahim. We actually looked quite similar, and since his first name was my last name, people often mistook us for each other. We laughed at that, and during the two years we attended the academy together—Lebanon's version of West Point—we became firm friends. After graduation, we were posted to different parts of the country, so we didn't see too much of each other. But our friendship remained strong and we often talked by telephone about our lives and the crisis in our country. We trusted each other, not just as friends but as comrades in arms during a very dangerous time.

This kind of bond lasts a lifetime. I went on to serve in the Eighth Brigade with General Michel Aoun, who went on to become the youngest-ever commander of the Lebanese Army. One time, a unit from the Israeli army tried to enter the zone I was in charge of protecting. We were under orders not to let any armed forces or factions into the area. I knew the Israelis could destroy my unit, but I told them that they would also lose many troops if they tried to force their way in. After a tense confrontation, they backed off. Abbas served in military intelligence and in a presidential military bodyguard unit, protecting presidents and high-ranking government officials through the 1990s. Sun Tzu shaped our military strategic thinking: "In the midst of chaos, there is also opportunity."

Eventually, though, I decided to leave Lebanon. For years, I had been fighting on so many different fronts, occupying foreign armies and local separatists' militias, and I decided it was time to build a new life in the United States, where I had the opportunity to train and graduate from its best military schools earlier in my military life. I proposed to my girlfriend, Sylvana—George Hajjar's sister—who lived in Texas, where there is a large Lebanese expat community. After we got married, we moved to El Paso, where I found work as a supply chain manager. God blessed Sylvana and me with two distinguished children, JJ and TC. In the summer of 2019, I was working on an assignment in Connecticut when I received the phone call about Sam from my brother-in-law, George.

My first thought was of my own kids, and what I would do if something bad happened to them. So I told George I would do what I could, but there was no way I could promise him anything.

"Let me make some calls," I told him.

Since I'd left Lebanon, my old commander from the Eighth Brigade, Michel Aoun, had gone on to great things. But it wasn't to him I turned when I heard of Sam's fate. If I was to approach the president, I would have to go in person to Lebanon. No, it was my old roommate Abbas Ibrahim. He was now a major general, with a long and storied career. In the mid-1990s, he had become head of counterterrorism and espionage operations. In 2011, he was appointed head of Lebanon's General Security Directorate, making him one of the most powerful people in the country. He was, in effect, Lebanon's fixer, its troubleshooter. He knew all the players, and they all trusted him. He had been the army's liaison with the various factions in implementing a UN resolution that ended the 2006 war with Israel and was also the intermediary in talks among Palestinian armed factions. He managed to straddle close ties with Washington and Damascus, and he is sought after as an effective and unofficial middleman by both sides. He is, in short, a key player in an often dangerous game of Middle East geopolitics.

Every time I went back to Lebanon to see my family, I would see the general. Our youthful friendship had matured into a deep mutual respect, even though our lives had taken us in very different directions. So I called him. He didn't answer immediately—he is a busy man—but he called me back within a few minutes.

"What's up?" he asked me. We speak rarely enough by phone these days that he knew something must have happened for me to just call out of the blue.

I told him what had happened.

"Send me his name and details, and a picture of his passport, so we know where to start," he said. "What does he do? Is he a spy or something? I need to know how to approach this."

"I don't know the kid," I said. "But his sister is friends with our kids. They're a good Catholic family like ours. I'll find out."

Via George, the Goodwins sent me all the information the general asked for. Abbas swore me to secrecy and said he would do what he could.

He contacted me less than two days later. I was getting off a flight in Rochester, New York, for a business meeting, and I had a message on my phone.

"We found your guy. He is alive."

I was on my way to pick up a rental car but immediately called him back. "The Syrians have him," he said. "We don't know more right now, but at least the guy is alive."

I hung up and called George. I didn't tell him my source, but George knows who I know. I told him it all had to remain strictly below the radar.

Then George relayed the good news to TAG and Ann. I don't think they quite believed it. After all, why would they? They were already a month into their ordeal, and the FBI, the CIA, the State Department, the Vatican, and regional NGOs had not been able to deliver a shred of concrete news as to where their son was. Then suddenly their daughter contacts an old college roommate and within two days they know their son is alive and with the Syrian regime. I probably wouldn't have believed it myself.

The general told me he was due in Damascus later that week on official business and would raise the issue with his high-level contacts there. From that point on, I was sure Sam would get out.

But General Ibrahim didn't make it to Syria that week.

While he was preparing for his trip, gunmen opened fire on the convoy of a government minister in a village close to Mount Lebanon. Two of his aides were killed, though he escaped unharmed. He described it as an assassination attempt against him, aimed at stoking tensions in the region.

As with most things in Lebanon's complex and often violent political world, the whole episode was a horrible mess. Another party claimed that the minister's own people had fired on a crowd of villagers who were blocking the road to protest a visit by Foreign Minister Gebran Bassil, who is the president's son-in-law, a Parliament representative, and a member of the Free Patriotic Movement. Yet another political faction said the shooting was actually an attempt planned on the life of the foreign minister.

The incident threatened to shatter the governing coalition and even spark renewed fighting. There was only one person who could sort it out—my friend General Ibrahim. He was locked into intense negotiations among the factions for the next two weeks, resulting in Sam Goodwin being pushed down the priority list and languishing in his jail cell.

Once he had managed to avert yet another potential war, General Ibrahim turned his attention back to Sam. This time, he traveled to Damascus to meet with Major General Ali Mamlouk, the head of Syria's National Security Bureau reporting directly to President Assad. Mamlouk is to Assad what the national security adviser is to American presidents.

"He is a spy," Mamlouk told General Ibrahim.

"No, he isn't. He is just a tourist. He's a nobody," insisted the general.

Mamlouk scoffed. "He's a spy. There are no tourists in Syria."

And he was right, almost. There are no tourists in Syria. Except for Sam.

SAM GOODWIN

At about nine in the evening on July 24, I was lying on my bunk, reading a dog-eared paperback that Elliot had given me. Elliot worked in the prison library and would bring me old English-language books to help pass the time.

This one was called *The Pledge* by Howard Fast, a mid-twentieth-century writer I'd never heard of, but who had in fact written the novel that became the legendary movie *Spartacus*. I was deep into the fast-paced thriller when the door of the cell opened. Everyone looked up at the guard as he entered our cell. He walked over to my bunk and told me to get my things together—we were leaving.

All of the other inmates came up to me and immediately started to congratulate me and give me hugs. "*Mabrouk*, Sam, you go home! Free! Mother, father, America," they said. I was confused. Was I really being let go all of a sudden?

The guard was waiting at the door as I packed up my meager belongings. Arthur went over to him to inquire about where I was going. When he came back a minute or two later, he looked worried.

He whispered to me. "I talked to the guard. You're being taken back to security."

No!

I felt the panic rising inside me. There was no way I could survive two stints in Branch 215 without being physically tortured. The sounds of the screams came back to me. I felt weak, shaky. I must have looked pale, because Arthur clasped me by the shoulders. "You are going to be okay, Sam. Trust in God."

That brought me back to my senses a bit. This was going to happen, whether I liked it or not, and it was happening right now. My friends and cellmates looked on, their celebration turning to shock. In the midst of the scene, I whispered to Arthur, asking him to tell Albert to tell Dinah to tell Steph that I was being moved from Adra. I had no idea if this message would make it to my family, but it was one of the few proactive measures I could take in the moment. I was definitely anxious as the guard escorted me out of the cell but forced my mind to cling to Arthur's departing words. *Trust in God.*

It was late, so instead of taking me straight back to Branch 215 that night, the guards put me in a holding pen at the front of Adra Prison with around forty other inmates who were also being spread out to whatever destination fate held in store for them. There were no beds here, and we clutched our minimal belongings as we lay on the bare concrete floor trying to snatch a few moments of sleep, trying not to think about what tomorrow would bring.

Early the next morning, we were chained together. The slave walk into the meat truck had become all too familiar by now, and we sat in silence in the back of that reeking vehicle as it made the rounds of Damascus's torture spots and covert human slaughterhouses, men being offloaded at each halt, until there was just me and a couple of others remaining.

I was offloaded and met by a security official on the side of a road. As we walked together around a building, I looked up and recognized the entrance to Branch 215. I was again seized by fear. In some ways, this was worse than when I had arrived here for the first time two months earlier. Back then, I had been racked by the uncertainty of what would happen to me. Now it was the certainty of what was going to happen to me that ate away at my spirit. I'd spent the last month hearing stories about all the horrors that went on in these facilities, which I had been able to hear but not see. This time, I knew what was in store for me.

"Looks like the judge was right and the inmates were wrong," I told myself as I was led inside, down the steps, and into the basement dungeon. There was an odd disconnect when the minions recognized me. They greeted me almost as they would an old friend and were pleasantly surprised when I answered them in Arabic, since I had learned basic phrases at Adra. Yet I believed these were the men who would soon be coming to my cell to drag me off to God knows what horrors.

They escorted me down the corridor to a cell. It was right next door to the cell I had left a month earlier when I was transferred to Adra.

I was shattered. As the metal door slammed shut behind me, I steeled myself for the worst, trying to dredge up the resolve to get myself back into the routine of isolation. At best, it seemed, the powers that be had decided I was a useful bargaining chip in whatever closed communications Damascus had with Washington, and I wasn't getting out anytime soon. At worst, they still thought I was a spy and were going to torture me until I confessed.

That afternoon of July 25, lying on an old wool blanket on the concrete floor, back in solitary confinement after a month at Adra, is the moment I consider to be the lowest point of my entire sixty-three days of captivity. In a somewhat remarkable paradox, at this exact same time, on the other side of the world and unbeknownst to me, my family received news that my release had been granted, a moment they consider to be their highest.

ANN GOODWIN

TAG and I scurried together across Charles de Gaulle Airport to the departing gate of the flight to Beirut. Joseph had been expecting an American couple, but it wasn't until I leaned on TAG that Joseph realized we were together. A Lebanese man in a business suit walked up to us and said, "Ann? TAG?"

I embraced him, we exchanged a few pleasantries, and I immediately asked if Sam was already out of Syria. Joseph dodged answering the question directly and tried to assure me of his trust in his friend. This was frustrating and made me question our decision to fly halfway around the world at the direction of "Joe from Connecticut," who was still unwilling to provide us with any concrete information. In addition, I recognized that if this channel didn't result in Sam's freedom, we were probably going to be back to square one, which could mean months before a new path was created. Several hours later, as our plane approached the eastern shore of the Mediterranean, I saw the city below. I was on edge.

After we landed, as our plane taxied from the runway to the jet bridge, the lead member of the cabin crew made an announcement over the intercom. "Ladies and gentlemen," she said, "once we park at the gate, we request that all passengers please remain seated."

A few minutes later, after the plane stopped, the woman came back on. "Mr. and Mrs. Goodwin, please collect your belongings and proceed to the exit of the aircraft."

A bit confused, we did as instructed and walked up the aisle of the plane while all other passengers stayed in their seats. When we stepped off, Joseph had already deboarded and was standing there with an army captain and several members of a Lebanese special forces unit. "Our escort," Joseph explained. "They will be with us the whole time we are here, until we board our flight home."

The officers whisked us through the diplomatic immigration channel. I had never gotten out of an airport so fast in my life, let alone when arriving internationally. Outside, there were three official black SUVs waiting for us. The captain explained that for security reasons, we were each assigned to travel in a separate vehicle. When Joseph saw my uneasiness with this arrangement, he got permission from the captain to ride with me, which I appreciated. TAG was placed in the vehicle behind us. We sped off and headed for what I learned to be the headquarters of Lebanon's General Security Directorate.

As we drove, given all that was happening, Joseph noticed my eyes tearing up. In response, he spoke in Arabic to the captain in the front seat. After a brief exchange that I couldn't understand, the captain made a phone call and handed the phone to Joseph, who then gave it to me.

Joseph told me to talk.

"Hello," I said into the phone.

A voice on the other end responded, "Welcome to Lebanon."

SAM GOODWIN

On my first morning back in the underground dungeon, before the daily screaming had begun, two guards came to fetch me and take me for a shower. This, again, was unusual in my experience of Branch

215, where I had only ever been allowed to shower late at night, except the one evening before I was going to be interrogated. When I had finished my perfunctory wash, I was led out of the dungeon and up the stairs again, back to the street level. A car was waiting for me outside. The guards loaded me into the back seat, no handcuffs or blindfold. This special treatment made me suddenly extremely nervous. Were they taking me somewhere worse than 215? Was I going to be executed?

The two men in the front of the car chatted to each other as we drove, scarcely paying any attention to me. I peered out at the city I had for so long wanted to visit, the bustling ancient hub of empires stretching back to antiquity. Everything seemed so normal—I could almost have been taking a cab ride as a tourist. Yet I didn't know if I was about to be killed, tortured, or thrown in another prison.

After a roughly fifteen-minute crosstown ride, the car pulled up to what looked like a government building. I was led inside to an office, where some men in suits who spoke passable English greeted me. They returned my broken phone, passport, and wallet, which quite remarkably still had all the cash in it. I was confused but accepted. Again, I saw that my phone had been disassembled into its smallest-possible parts and was unusable. Then, to my complete surprise, they brought in a large platter of rice and meat, more food than I had seen in months. They invited me to dig in, which I did with a voracious appetite, not knowing when I might get another meal.

As we finished eating, one of the Syrian officials looked at me and said, "Sam, you're very lucky. President Assad has agreed to release you."

I didn't say anything. With every fiber in my body, I wanted this to be true, but I had been lied to so many times in the past two months that I had essentially become immune to believing anything like this. I can't even remember what I said in response, I was so busy trying to master the roller coaster of emotions his words threatened to unleash.

A few minutes later, a man in a uniform walked into the room and started speaking to the officials in Arabic. His uniform looked different from the ones I'd seen up until now. I looked closer and saw a Lebanese flag patch on his shoulder—the distinctive green cedar tree on a white background, with a red stripe at the top and bottom. Suddenly, all the pent-up hope inside me welled up. I interrupted the conversation he was having with the Syrian officials.

"You're from Lebanon?" I blurted out.

He smiled and responded in a friendly, slightly sarcastic tone.

"Yeah, I'm gonna take you there today. Do you want to come?"

I wasn't sure if he was serious. I couldn't even be sure he was actually Lebanese or part of some elaborate hoax being played on me. But of course, I said yes. He finished talking to the Syrians, then led me outside to where a black SUV was waiting. He got in the front while I sat in the back, next to a huge man in military fatigues and with arms so muscular he looked like Popeye. No one said a word as the car—one of five matching black SUVs in our convoy—pulled out and sped at what felt like a hundred miles per hour through the streets of Damascus. We didn't stop at traffic lights or junctions, and whenever there was a buildup of traffic, the convoy simply swung onto the hard shoulder and shot past the jams.

As we left the city, I could tell we were headed west, toward the mountains. Still, nobody said a word, but the flashy cars and professional nature of the men around me gave me the sense that things were either really good or really bad. It seemed as though I was about to experience one end of the "captivity spectrum," but I was still unsure which it would be.

About an hour into our drive, we approached what seemed to be a major checkpoint. We slowed down but were waved through, given the official nature of our convoy. As we passed through the barriers, I could see it was a border crossing. Popeye tapped me on the leg and quietly said, "Sam, you're in Lebanon. You're safe now."

Just as it had been hard, months earlier, for me to tell that I had been captured, it was now hard for me to tell if I had been rescued, even though all the evidence suggested I had been. I waited a few minutes to ask the unit commander in the front seat what happened now. Would they just open the door in Beirut and drop me off, or would I be put in prison in Lebanon? I had no idea.

Now that we were clear of Syria, the commander finally introduced himself as Fawzi. "Sam, we're taking you to a hotel in Beirut so you can take a shower," he said. "Then we're going to my boss's office … and your parents might be there."

This was all a bit too much to take in, coming just hours after I had been sent back to one of the worst prisons in the world. But I had been without agency for so long, at the mercy of forces out of my control, that all I could do was sit passively in the car and wait to see whether my deliverance was really at hand.

The convoy was traveling at a more normal speed now. It's almost an hour's drive from the Syrian border to Beirut. I watched as the beautiful scenery flashed past, the small towns and villages, and I could feel myself slowly coming back to life, fresh shoots of hope and curiosity springing from nerve endings I had been forced to deaden while in captivity.

When we finally got to Beirut, I was stunned to see the hotel we were moving into—the InterContinental Phoenicia, right on the Mediterranean, one of the finest hotels in the entire country. It had been far beyond my budget when I had visited Lebanon as a traveler eight months earlier. Now, Fawzi and Popeye—whose real name I had by now learned was Georgio—escorted me inside to an opulent room with a balcony overlooking the water. They waited as I shaved and took a shower. When I emerged, clean and refreshed, Georgio told me we had a few minutes to spare before we had to go to the office of his boss. Given the delay, I asked him if I could borrow his phone. He nodded. I took the phone and stepped out onto the balcony. My first instinct was to try to make a phone call to my family, but I wasn't sure if that was off-limits and didn't want to cause any trouble. So, with access to the internet for the first time in nine weeks, I opened YouTube and typed in "2019 Stanley Cup Final." The first video to pop up had been posted online six weeks earlier. When I read the title, I thought to myself, "Oh my gosh, they won. There must have been a parade in St. Louis."

As I was looking out over the beautiful cityscape of Beirut and the sparkling sea, Georgio stepped out beside me on the balcony. "A few hours ago I was eating a hard-boiled egg off the concrete floor of a Damascus prison cell, and now I'm in a five-star hotel overlooking the Mediterranean Sea," I said to him, shaking my head in total disbelief. "What a morning."

"It's time to go," said Georgio.

On the drive across town, Georgio explained to me that my parents were in fact in Beirut. I had come to view him as trustworthy and was also beginning to truly believe that I was free. Georgio indicated that things might get very emotional and that I should try to be strong so that my mom didn't break down too much when we met. He proceeded to call his colleague who was driving my parents to see if they were on their way, then handed me the phone.

"It's your mother," he said.

I tried to be strong and not "overly emotional," even though I just wanted to scream with joy. So I tried to sound casual.

"Welcome to Lebanon," was the best I could come up with.

The headquarters of Lebanon's General Security Directorate looks like something out of ancient Egypt, a modern interpretation of a temple in the Valley of the Kings. It's a giant, stone-clad box that rises above the city of Beirut, with a few square windows and some pillars out front, over the heavily guarded entranceway.

We came in a side entrance, quickly waved through in our convoy, before being whisked to an office suite on the top floor. There were two people waiting for me in the room. One of them stepped forward to shake my hand.

"Hi, Sam, I'm Anish, the FBI attaché at the US embassy in Lebanon. Welcome to Beirut. There are many people back in Washington who are so happy you're safe."

I shook his hand enthusiastically, overwhelmed with gratitude and relief. I had never in my life met an FBI agent before. As Anish and I were talking, the office door burst open and my parents appeared. It was an indescribable moment of joy in the office. My mom rushed straight for me and embraced me in a huge hug, tears streaming down her face. Then my dad wrapped me in his arms and held me for a long time. It was a moment that I learned many people thought would never happen and frankly a breathtaking display of God answering prayers.

Before our conversation went any further, my mom asked me if I had come across another American, the journalist Austin Tice. Unfortunately, I had not and wasn't able to offer any information. Then my dad introduced me to another man who had come in with them, and whom I had barely noticed in the outburst of joy.

"Do you remember Steph's roommate at Belmont?" my dad asked. It was a very odd thing to be asked in that setting. In addition, during my sister's entire time at college, I had been living and working in Singapore, so I confessed that I essentially had no recollection of Stephanie Hajjar. "Well, this is her uncle," my dad said.

I was completely mystified by this point, wondering why on earth my parents had brought my sister's former college roommate's uncle with them to Beirut for my release from a Syrian prison.

"Sam, meet Joseph," my dad said. "Joseph helped get you out of Syria."

Joseph gave me a brief rundown of the extraordinary circumstances that had led us all to this government security headquarters in Beirut—how the two Stephanies had become college friends because they shared the same first name and Catholic belief, and how, forty years earlier, Lebanese Army recruits Joseph Abbas and Abbas Ibrahim had shared the same name and a dormitory in Beirut's military academy, leading to a lifelong friendship. If my sister hadn't happened to have met a total stranger in her first week of college, or if that girl's uncle had been assigned to a different dorm in the 1980s, I would likely still be trapped in a Syrian dungeon, wrongfully accused of spying for the United States. Clearly, God had a plan from the beginning.

The only thing I could think of to say was, "Thank you," and I meant it with all my heart.

Then the door opened again and a fit-looking man in his fifties, wearing a smart suit and blue tie, walked in. It was immediately clear from his demeanor that he was the master of this place, General Abbas Ibrahim himself.

He greeted his old friend Joseph, who introduced us to him. My mom asked if it was okay if she hugged him. The general clearly wasn't used to this kind of response—this is a man who had to deal with Hezbollah and the Syrians on a daily basis—but he took it in stride. Mom gave him a big hug, tears in her eyes, and thanked him as only a mother can when she has been reunited with her lost son.

Then it was my turn. Again, all I could say in that moment was the most direct thing I felt. "*Shukran*," I said, shaking his hand. "Thank you."

I later learned that the American official who typically greets freed hostages and who would under most circumstances have been in that office is the US government's SPEHA. But on the same day I was released, Robert O'Brien was in Stockholm dealing with A$AP Rocky. Two days later, however, Robert flew to Beirut to personally thank Abbas Ibrahim for his work on my case.

In the office, we all talked for a little while, and the general told us we were free to leave Lebanon anytime. It turned out my parents hadn't booked return tickets, not knowing if I would actually be released. That was when we made a collective decision to spend the night in Beirut to allow everyone to decompress, and then fly back to the United States in the morning.

"I know you've been to Lebanon before," Joseph said to me. "Is there anything you missed last time that you'd still like to see?"

I thought about it for a minute. It seemed so strange to be contemplating sightseeing when just that morning I'd been wondering if I was going to be tortured. Then I remembered a place I had read about that I hadn't had time to visit before.

"Up in the mountains there's this famous monastery named for a Lebanese monk…"

I stopped, because they were all looking at me in utter disbelief.

ANN GOODWIN

Aside from the bliss of having Sam back and holding him in my arms, there is another thing that remains in my memory of that joyful reunion in General Ibrahim's office.

After the hugs and tears, we were talking over cups of tea. The general told us a little bit about how he got Sam out. Apparently, when General Ibrahim was trying to negotiate with his Syrian counterpart, Ali Mamlouk, to release Sam, he had to convince him that Sam was just a traveler, of no interest to the regime.

"Let me have this guy, he's a nobody, he's not a terrorist, he's not a spy, he's just a nobody, let me have this one," he told the Syrian spymaster.

What General Ibrahim didn't know was that President Assad himself was in a room next door and overheard the conversation. He stepped in and interrupted.

"Well, considering he's a nobody, everybody seems to want him," the Syrian dictator said. "The Vatican wants him. The patriarch wants him. Doctors Without Borders want him. The Russians want him too. Even the Czechs want him. That's quite a 'nobody.'"

It was a stunning revelation. There we had been, sending out feelers like tracer bullets in the dark, never knowing if any had even hit their mark. And it turned out that *many* had reached President Assad. True, they could all have resulted in nothing, and probably would have without that miracle of my daughter's phone call to her former roommate, but our message had gotten through. People had actually gone the full nine yards and passed on our plea, through half a dozen different channels, to the Syrian leader himself.

Six degrees of separation. I counted them off on my fingers— Steph, Stephanie, Joseph Abbas, General Ibrahim, Ali Mamlouk, Bashar al-Assad. Exactly six degrees between an ordinary family in St. Louis, Missouri, and the president of Syria. Astounding.

After the meeting wound up, our special forces escort took us back to the hotel. For the first time, TAG and I were alone with our son and we could really tell each other how we were feeling—elated, relieved, exhausted, full of love, and grateful to God that Sam was with us, apparently unharmed, though about twelve pounds lighter.

Sam came over to me. "There's something I need to tell you, and I wasn't sure I'd ever get the chance. Thank you for teaching me how to pray. I wouldn't have made it through the past few months without my faith." And he started to cry, the first time I'd seen him do that since he was a child.

I smiled at him. "I always knew miracles were real," I said. "I just didn't know God would do one for me."

SAM GOODWIN

The shrine of Saint Charbel is a beautiful stone monastery located on a mountaintop overlooking the Mediterranean Sea. Beneath it, on the coast, is the ancient city of Byblos. The site has been inhabited for some ten thousand years and the city used to ship papyri around the ancient Mediterranean world, hence the Greek word *biblio*, for "book," from which we derive the word *bible*.

The place is officially called the Monastery of Saint Maron—who gave his name to Lebanese Catholicism, the Maronite Church—but these days it is probably more famous for the miracle-working Saint

Charbel, who lived a life of solitude and prayer here for twenty-three years until his death in 1898.

Joseph acted as our guide. His family lives near Byblos, and we stopped by his parents' house on our way to the monastery. They had only just learned their son was even in Lebanon and were further befuddled when he arrived to their street with a five-vehicle convoy of black SUVs and two dozen special forces acting as an escort. Taking it all in stride, they welcomed us into their home, while most of the soldiers stayed outside, and opened a bottle of Kefraya wine to celebrate the return of prodigal sons.

On top of the mountain, Joseph showed us around the sprawling monastery complex. For me, the most striking part was the bare cell where Saint Charbel spent his days in prayer. It wasn't too dissimilar from the cell I had been in just a few hours earlier—a goat-hair blanket on the flagstone floor and a block of wood for a pillow, covered by a scrap of cloth from an old monastic robe. In these unforgiving surroundings, he had come closer to God, just as I had over the previous nine weeks in Syria.

Walking out of the monastery, we were met by our special forces guards again. My mom apologized to Georgio, who had been part of my escort out of Damascus earlier that day.

"I'm sorry to keep you from your family, Georgio. You should be at home by now, not showing us around."

Georgio insisted he didn't mind. "I like coming to this place," he said. He then told my mom that he often came here anyway to give thanks for a miracle.

Of course, this comment piqued our interest and we asked him to share the story. Georgio explained that a few years earlier, he had been in a serious car accident. Tragically, his fiancée was killed, while Georgio was left paralyzed from the waist down and needing a wheelchair. Two and a half months after the crash, his parents brought him here to the Saint Charbel monastery to pray for a cure. He recounted to us that, following his prayer, he stood up, walked out of the church, and left the wheelchair at the monastery.

We were captivated by this story, one that was compounded by all that had already happened that day. We learned that Saint Charbel is celebrated for thousands of such miracles. In fact, more than twenty-nine thousand miracles are attributed to Saint Charbel, more than any other saint in the history of the church besides Mary. It was said that after he died, his body did not decay. Between 1950 and 1975, the monastery allowed doctors to open his tomb eight times to carry out tests on his remains. They said the body appeared to still be largely as it was when he died just before the turn of the century, but they could offer no medical explanation for the phenomenon. His reputation has since drawn millions of visitors to the monastery overlooking the sea.

That evening, we drove down to Byblos for dinner at a restaurant by the Mediterranean. Lebanese food is one of my favorite cuisines, and after being in prison for months, it tasted extra delicious that evening. When we got back to Beirut, it was late and we were all exhausted but at peace with the world and its miraculous happenings.

When we returned to the hotel, I was astonished to see that my parents had brought with them my North Face backpack. I had written it off weeks earlier and had a lot of questions about how they possibly could have retrieved it. I had some trouble falling asleep that evening given the softness of the hotel bed. My body had adapted to a concrete floor. The following morning, my parents and I, accompanied by Anish and another FBI agent, flew home to St. Louis.

EPILOGUE

ANN GOODWIN

There are probably no words to adequately describe the gratitude of reuniting with a lost child after an ordeal like Sam's. But as we would soon learn, Saint Charbel, the miracle-working Lebanese monk, wasn't quite finished with us yet.

The day after Sam returned home, as our family was still savoring the joy Betty described as "Christmas morning," TAG stepped into another room of our house to answer an unexpected phone call from a Canadian woman. She said she saw the news of Sam's release and indicated that her son had been missing in Syria for the past eight months. She explained that she's a single mother with only one child. The desperation in her voice was clear. TAG asked what efforts she had been making to try to find her son. She explained that the Canadian government up to this point had been unhelpful and obviously unsuccessful, and therefore she felt all she could do was pray.

Her son was forty-four-year-old Kristian Baxter, who had gone to Syria as a traveler in November 2018. Within a week of his arrival, he vanished. Kristian, like Sam, was also being wrongfully held on bogus charges.

Of course, we wanted to do everything we could to help this Canadian mother. Via Joseph, TAG reached back out to General Ibrahim and described the situation to him. Enigmatic as ever, he said he would make some inquiries and see what he could do. On August 9, 2019, exactly two weeks after Sam's release, Kristian Baxter walked free from Syria. At a small press conference in Beirut, flanked by General Ibrahim and the Canadian ambassador, he fought back tears as he thanked the Lebanese government for helping to free him. "I thought I would be there forever, honestly," Kristian said.

In our prayers, we often implore God to use us as he sees fit, even though we rarely know the details of what he has in store. Why was Sam wrongfully taken in Syria? I believe he was being used as God's instrument. Sam was an innocent and well-intentioned traveler, and certainly didn't deserve to be unjustly accused of espionage. But if he had not been kidnapped, and a path not created for his release, Kristian would potentially still be in captivity and his mother would be going through all the pain and uncertainty we suffered, perhaps for the rest of her life. I believe God used Sam, and our family, to free Kristian Baxter, and we were all made vastly stronger for it.

As it turns out, that renowned phone call between the Stephanies actually led to the release of *two* hostages.

SAM GOODWIN

As my parents and I made the journey home from Beirut to St. Louis, we tracked the news of my release breaking on networks around the world. I didn't have a working phone, so my parents shared messages they were receiving from family and friends. On the plane, my dad showed me an email from David Bradley, who I quickly learned had been instrumental in supporting my family.

Hi TAG and Ann,

I don't know if you know already how seldom there's been any good news out of Syria. Your rescue of Sam is remarkable. I am so glad for him, and so glad for the two of you.

I suspect that this will be the great story of your lifetime. If they make a movie about you, this will be the best scene. I wish I could be there to see you and to meet Sam.

I wish you safe travels home. The eagle has landed.

David

When we touched down at St. Louis's Lambert Airport on the evening of July 27, the FBI had arranged for my siblings and Rob Martini to meet us immediately at the gate, like in pre-9/11 times. Arriving back on US soil was a breathtaking reminder of how grateful and fortunate I am to be American. I was greeted with big hugs, in addition to wry and on-brand comments from my siblings.

"Damn, you look skinny," Paul said. I laughed.

Betty added, "Welcome home! You look tired."

I replied, "Yeah…near-death experiences have that effect."

When we arrived back at our parents' house, the perimeter of the front lawn had been lit up by brown paper bags with candles in them laid out by my aunt Christi, my mom's sister, as a homecoming gesture. I learned that Christi had prayed a novena for me every hour for sixty-three days. That night, we all stayed up late and kicked off what would become months of discussion around the unforgettable saga of the summer of 2019. The following morning, we went to eleven o'clock Sunday Mass together at St. Clement. As we parked our car and walked to the church, my family pointed at the adoration chapel and told me the story of the gathering there at two in the morning. After Mass, TAG received a phone call from Abbas Ibrahim, who was kindly checking in to ensure we didn't have any travel issues and had all made it back safely to St. Louis.

Among my first meals back in the United States was of course Chipotle. Unfortunately, a few days later I ended up in the emergency room because of stomach pain. Turns out, during those nine weeks of captivity, my body had adapted to the low-calorie prison diet and was essentially shocked when confronted with a burrito, in addition to all the other Western food I was feeding it. In my case, a routine antibiotic did the trick, but this episode continues to make me wonder what other returning hostages could experience after being held for much longer, sometimes years. Over the coming days, as I decompressed and recovered from my stomach issue, I took time to watch reruns of the Blues' Stanley Cup games. I was also experiencing some mild episodes of PTSD, particularly when going to sleep at night, but thankfully, for the most part, I've been able to address these instances with a robust support system of family and friends, as well as prayer. It may be a hot take, but I think Catholics figured out therapy two thousand years ago. That first week home also included some interesting conversations with my bank as I attempted to convince them that being held hostage in a foreign country is grounds for them to forgive credit card late fees—unfortunately to no avail. All of these things collectively, among others, are elements of learning to "survive survival," which I discovered, and continue to discover, is an intricate and long-standing process.

Two days after arriving home, as the true realization of a peaceful ending was beginning to set in on all of us, I was walking down a small hallway of my parents' house from the kitchen into the family room. Steph happened to be walking the other direction at the same time. As we passed each other, neither of us breaking stride, I quietly and subtly said, "Steph, thanks for getting me out of Syria." In the same tone and without skipping a beat, she replied, "Yeah, sure, anytime."

About a week later, I spent several days debriefing with the FBI. I learned from them that I had become the only American civilian ever to be released from captivity by the Assad regime. They told me that the information I had obtained could potentially help them with other hostage cases, which led to me happily sharing every detail with them I could possibly remember about life inside Assad's network of dungeons. In a bit of twisted irony, the Syrians arrested a simple traveler as a suspected spy and threw me in prison, which led to me becoming a de facto spy for the US government after the fact.

I'm unsure whether my feedback to the FBI was actually helpful, but they continue to tell me it was.

Among the most overwhelming things for me in the aftermath of my captivity was, and continues to be, learning about all the people who were involved in helping to bring me home—from people who loved me to people who had no idea who I was—none of which I knew anything about while I was detained. Today, several years later, I'm still saying thank you, and I'm sure I will continue doing so. I consider the entire SG23 team to be family, including Stephanie Hajjar, whom I call my "Lebanese guardian angel." I make routine trips to Toronto to see Rob, whose son Max is my godson, and to Miami to visit Father Vigoa, whom my family now recognizes as our own family priest. Speaking of the Catholic Church, in September 2023, I caught up with Cardinal Zenari at the nunciature in DC while he was on an official visit to the United States. He gave me a big hug and expressed his relief that I was home safe. I asked him about his arms, which I learned he had injured in the summer of 2019. He appreciated the gesture and said he had recovered from the fall. He then said with a smirk, "I survived the entire Syria war but then got hurt in Italy—go figure."

In September 2019, I met up with Joss in Brooklyn. We had dinner together and reminisced about all that had happened since our discussion in Fiji that May. She filled me in on her travels, particularly getting detained and deported from Iran and the final stretch of her Total World Tour, while I of course gave her the scoop on what had transpired in Syria and the details of how things had gone sideways. We were both thrilled that all had been resolved peacefully.

In December 2022, Joss hosted my sister Steph and me backstage during her concert at the Ryman Auditorium in Nashville. Joss is a fantastic performer, friend, and now, mother. We remain in touch today and connect when our schedules intersect.

Robert O'Brien went on to be promoted from chief hostage envoy to US national security adviser in September 2019, a role he held until the end of the Trump administration. He kindly welcomed my mom and me to the White House in late 2019 and our entire family in October 2020. On his desk was the travel photo scrapbook my parents had given him during my captivity. Not only had he kept this, but he had brought it with him from his State Department office to his White House office. He also gave me my "baseball card," which I still have today.

In addition to Robert, I've come to know many of the US government folks who worked on my case, including Paul Osborne. Although I learned that my family's experience with them during my captivity was a bit of a roller coaster, lots of them have become close friends. They are top-notch people and we could not be more grateful for the efforts of every single one of them. In August 2020, President Trump invited me, along with five other former hostages, to the White House. Chatting with the president of the United States was memorable, and I remain thankful for the invitation and opportunity.

Abbas Ibrahim continues to make routine trips to DC. Despite his busy schedule, he consistently makes time for the Goodwins when he's in town. My family and I are forever indebted to him for his efforts to free me. In 2023, he retired from his post as Lebanese intelligence chief. It's currently unclear what his next professional step may be, but some speculate he has further political aspirations.

Since I was freed, many of my fellow inmates from Adra have also been released. Some are now living in Damascus, while others have fled to neighboring Lebanon and Turkey, or into Europe. As these men trickle out of Adra and begin rebuilding their lives, they often reach out to me, typically by sending a friend request on social media. When I receive these requests, I often notice that we have as many as fifteen to twenty mutual friends. It's a humorous but also humbling reminder that I'm part of the Adra club. One of them recently invited me to his upcoming wedding in Damascus, but I unfortunately don't think I'm going to make it.

In the summer of 2021, my mom and I went to Gaziantep in Turkey, close to the Syrian border, and met with Albert, who is now working there in a furniture factory. It was a remarkable experience to be together as free men after having met inside a Syrian prison. My mother was in tears as she thanked him for communicating with our family via his sister. In addition to the inmates I met personally, Omar Alshogre and I have become friends and frequently attend events together, speaking on panels to advocate for the plight of the Syrian people, especially those held in regime-run detention centers. Omar works for the Syrian Emergency Task Force (SETF), a DC-based advocacy organization whose staff, particularly Mouaz Moustafa, continues to be incredibly helpful to me in navigating all that has come with the aftermath of captivity.

Arthur is still in prison. His sentence was unfortunately and seemingly inexplicably adjusted to a life sentence, which is infuriating. The only silver lining is that in 2021 he was reassigned from Adra to Sweida Prison, in the south of the country, a facility in which inmates are allowed to have mobile phones. I WhatsApp with Arthur frequently and pray that something with his case changes soon and we can reunite. He frequently expresses his frustration and hopelessness to me, to which I've found myself replying with the same words of wisdom he offered me when I was being transferred from Adra back to Branch 215—*Trust in God.*

Whenever I speak with my old cellmates, I ask them if they have seen or heard any sign of Austin Tice. Unfortunately, to date, I have not been able to identify any leads via their channels. In addition to Austin, there are reportedly a handful of other Americans being held in Syria too. I often wonder if the same man who interrogated me also interrogated them. In any case, for several reasons, I would be eager to meet him again someday, assuming the handcuffs and blindfold are left at home.

Despite all that happened in Syria, my original curiosity about the world had never been stronger. Syria was country 181 of 193, and after several weeks of reflection and taking the time to begin putting things into context, I became eager to continue pursuing my travel goal. Travel was therapeutic, as it was a way for me to return to what I had been doing before and, most important, a way to not let what happened in Syria conquer me.

Of the twelve remaining countries, eleven were simple for Americans to visit, mostly Caribbean islands. The one potential hiccup was Venezuela, a country that has experienced political turmoil in recent years. But over Thanksgiving 2019, I spent five days in Venezuela, a country I discovered to be among the most naturally beautiful in the world. I camped at the base of Angel Falls, the highest waterfall on earth, and went for several long canoe rides on the Churún River. It became one of the best travel experiences I've ever had.

A month later, on December 31, 2019, I landed in Rio de Janeiro, Brazil, country 193 of 193. That evening, I rang in the new year, and new decade, on Copacabana Beach alongside more than three million people, one of the largest public gatherings anywhere in the world. I was filled with gratitude and overwhelmed as I watched the fireworks and reflected on all that had transpired throughout my journey. In early 2024, for good measure, I made a trip to Antarctica, marking my visit to continent seven of seven. Today, Rob enjoys making the snarky but somewhat amusing comment to me, "Sam, congratulations, you traveled to all 193 countries in the world and only went to prison in one of them. That's a great batting average!"

I flew home from Rio to St. Louis in January 2020. A few weeks later, COVID-19 hit, which for me meant isolation 2.0. I found it interesting to see national TV networks bringing former hostages and prisoners of war onto their shows to talk about how to cope with feeling trapped.

In March 2020, just before the world shut down entirely, I was invited to Fort Bragg in North Carolina to brief a group of seventy-five Green Berets and special forces operatives. They run a training course called Survival, Evasion, Resistance, and Escape (SERE), which is administered to officers who are put on missions where they may be at risk of being captured. A key component of the course is learning how to stay physically and emotionally strong if held in solitary confinement or facing torture in an enemy prison. Since I had been dropped into that very situation without any training, I was seemingly a useful example for them. I described how I had coped and which practices really helped me. As it turned out, I had instinctively done several of the key things they teach in their program—establish a routine, mark the passage of time, and try to keep physically fit. Control what you can control, and try not to stress too much about the things out of your control. Many of these skills I attribute to a career as a competitive athlete. Establishing communication with home, I said, had also been a vital element in keeping my hopes alive. The key for me, I told them, had been my faith and my determination to see my family again, to spare them the horror of not knowing what had happened to me.

In the summer of 2020, given the lockdown, I opted to go to graduate school and began a master's in international affairs at Washington University in St. Louis. I wrote my capstone thesis about the ongoing conflict in Syria and used several of my friends from Adra as primary sources in the paper. When I had arrived back in St. Louis in January 2020, I had a lot to chew on—Singapore, 193, Syria, and so on. Going back to school truly helped me get back on track. I completed my master's in the fall of 2021 and moved on to a doctorate program, also in international affairs, at Johns Hopkins University School of Advanced International Studies. Since August 2022 and up to the time of this writing, I've been living in DC and enjoy being at the heart of the policymaking world. Luke and other DC-based members of the SG23 operation are dear friends and I see them frequently. I go to class every day with my North Face backpack, a bag that I've calculated has traveled with me to every single country. I occasionally wonder if it's the most traveled North Face product ever...

In the fall of 2021, Michael Spavor and Michael Kovrig were released from prison in China after two years and ten months. I was overjoyed to hear the news. Several months later, I reconnected with Michael Spavor and flew to Calgary to see him. We recapped our detention stories and compared Chinese and Syrian prisons. We enjoyed reflecting on the trajectory of our friendship—meeting in North Korea, both being unjustly detained by hostile foreign governments, both being released, and now both having breakfast together in Canada. Michael and I continue to support each other as we navigate our own reintegration processes.

Since 2019, I've become and remain committed to using my experiences to help and support the community of other Americans who are being held hostage or wrongfully detained overseas. In 2022, I was hired for a fellowship by the James W. Foley Legacy Foundation to do advocacy work on Capitol Hill, lobbying members of Congress to take action on these issues. It's a privilege to know and work alongside Diane Foley, who experienced the unimaginable and has become stronger as a result. I coauthored a *Traveler Safety Guide* that the foundation published to help Americans travel better and safer, and I remain on the advisory council of the organization. In March 2023, Diane and I took our hostage advocacy work overseas, having been invited by Ali Soufan to speak on a panel at his Global Security Forum in Doha.

In the aftermath of my release, my family and I resisted media interviews for over a year and a half. We wanted to take our time to reflect and do our best to put things into perspective. In January 2021, we finally opened up publicly about some of the details of the saga and agreed to do a story with the *Wall Street Journal*, a piece that ran as a Saturday-edition page one feature. Robert O'Brien went on record saying, "What the Goodwin family did was extraordinary." Joss added, "I felt personally responsible. Logic says it isn't your fault, but your heart says it is." Abbas Ibrahim contributed by affectionately saying, "I have a soft spot for mothers." My family and I remain open to continuing to share our experiences and what we learned through them. This book is a step in that direction.

In the wake of the *Wall Street Journal* story, I received a spontaneous message via social media from a woman who disclosed that she and her family are relatives of Elliot and were the ones who had called TAG to relay information about the salmon note. They are a Syrian American family and now live, of all places, in St. Louis. After a few text exchanges, my mom and I met up with them for dinner, at the Missouri Athletic Club, in fact. They explained to us that after receiving the note from Elliot and learning about my case, they wanted to help but were simultaneously cautious about getting too involved, particularly because some of their family still lives in Syria and they didn't want to do anything that might jeopardize their security. They therefore used the app magicJack to call TAG, which includes a feature allowing users to make calls while controlling their ID settings. This is why the phone number came up as a Florida area code. It turns out, that Sunday morning phone call to TAG was physically made from less than five miles away.

This Syrian American family remains friends of ours today, and they often apologize for having had to be so cryptic on the phone in 2019.

In the spring of 2023, Niagara University invited me to be their commencement speaker. I had only been back to campus one time since graduating in 2012, so it was an honor to return to my undergrad alma mater, especially in that context, and reunite with former professors and coaches. I spoke to the graduates about the ups and downs of my experience as an entrepreneur in Singapore, what I learned through travel, and the best ways to manage the inevitable feeling in life of being trapped—the key takeaways being gratitude, curiosity, and faith.

～

I don't hate my prison guards. I don't hate my interrogator. I don't even hate the man in the white soccer jersey in Qamishli who I believe determined and sealed my fate as a political hostage in Syria. I've forgiven all of them, and I hope someday they're able to free themselves from the ideologies of a corrupt regime. Everyone deserves freedom, even them.

I could play the victim card forever, and probably do so successfully, but what good would that do? In the years since my release, my goal with this experience has evolved into a twofold mission. The first is to raise awareness for these issues so there's never another Sam Goodwin in Syria, so this doesn't ever happen to another American anywhere in the world. The second is to identify the key lessons I've learned through this experience and share them with others in a relatable way.

Some doctors and psychologists who studied American POWs from Vietnam say that those men are healthier today, mentally and physically, than if they'd never been shot down. Similarly, people often ask me today, "Sam, if you could go back, would you still travel the way you did and still go to Syria?" On one hand, I would never want to relive captivity and wouldn't wish that on anyone. On the other hand, and more important, I would never want to give up everything that's come from it—the opportunity to meet some remarkable people and to grow in character, faith, and understanding of things in life that actually matter. And those two things go together, making this question genuinely challenging to answer.

Over the past several years, I've delivered hundreds of keynote presentations to organizations across the United States and beyond, primarily at corporate conferences and conventions. My central message is around *embracing uncertainty*. In captivity, I was pushed to a point of overwhelming uncertainty, truly life or death. But through that, I learned some things—some things that have helped me and some things that I know can help others too when they're facing uncertainty in their own personal and professional lives.

I view the world through a spiritual lens, and I believe God gave me this experience in Syria for a reason. I don't feel so much survivor's guilt as I do survivor's responsibility—an obligation to use all I've been given to effect some sort of positive change in the world. I'm humbled by the responses I receive from people in audiences today who say that I brought them hope, or gratitude, or a new perspective on the world. I love my speaking business and its impact, not to mention that it has also allowed me to fulfill the promise I made to myself when I left Singapore in 2018—that I would go back to my career. It's been a circuitous route and I never could have anticipated public speaking being my next career move, but I wouldn't change a thing. I believe that in life when we feel the most lost, we often have the best chance for a huge breakthrough. As an athlete, entrepreneur, traveler, and hostage, I can tell you there is value and opportunity in every experience.

I expect the lessons I learned in captivity to stay with me in some shape or form for the rest of my life. While Syria doesn't define me, it has become a part of who I am. Many people said my life was over, but in truth, it was just getting going.

ACKNOWLEDGMENTS

As the finishing touches were being put on this book, my editor asked, "Sam, do you want to add an acknowledgments section?" I responded by saying that I feel as though this entire book is one big acknowledgments section. Truly, as I've said many times, I could not be more grateful for everyone in this story who played a role in providing me with what I consider to be a second chance at life.

For this project specifically, though, I must first say thanks to James Hider, who spent hours interviewing the various narrators and consolidating the information. James, this book would simply not exist without you. My family and I appreciate all the work you did to help bring our story to the world.

Alex Pappas, you and the Center Street team have been a pleasure to work with. I am a first-time author, so the publishing space was like a giant black hole to me. Thank you for being so patient, supportive, and creative, and always taking the time to answer my endless questions. I couldn't have asked for a better editor and publisher.

I want to give a special mention to my younger brother Paul, whose voice was not heard in first person in the book but who played many key roles in supporting the SG23 efforts. Paul, I'm confident that the story of you arriving to the meeting with Archbishop Auza in New York will forever be one of Father Vigoa's all-time favorites.

Lastly, I want to thank my mom. No doubt, my whole family and network of friends were remarkably supportive throughout this process, but nobody spent as much time and effort helping me write as she did. She's my biggest critic and was always the first to tell me when I wrote something dumb but also the first to tell me when something was great. Flan, this book would not be the same without you.

It turns out, rescuing a hostage and writing a book both require the collaborative effort of an exceptional team, each of whom leaves their own enduring mark. Thank you to everyone who has been part of this unforgettable journey.

ABOUT THE AUTHOR

Sam Goodwin is an American entrepreneur, author, and public speaker. A former Division I collegiate hockey player, he is one of the few people who have traveled to all 193 countries in the world and also the only American civilian to be released from captivity by the Assad regime. As an international keynote speaker, Sam and his message have inspired audiences and added value to hundreds of organizations around the world. Goodwin grew up in St. Louis, Missouri, and currently lives in Washington, DC, where he earned a doctorate in international affairs from Johns Hopkins SAIS and serves on the boards of multiple advocacy organizations.